Hillary
C L I N T O N

IN HER OWN WORDS

Edited by Lisa Rogak

SEAL PRESS

ISBN 978-1-58005-533-8
Library of Congress Cataloging-in-Publication Data

Hillary Clinton in her own words / [edited by] Lisa Rogak.
    pages cm
 ISBN 978-1-58005-533-8
1. Clinton, Hillary Rodham--Quotations. 2. Presidential
candidates--United States--Quotations. 3. Legislators--United
States--Quotations. 4. Women legislators--United States--Quotations. 5.
Presidents' spouses--United States--Quotations. I. Rogak, Lisa, 1962-
  E887.C55H53 2014
  328.73'092--dc23
  [B]

                        2013047515

Published by
Seal Press
A Member of the Perseus Books Group
1700 Fourth Street
Berkeley, California
sealpress.com

Cover and interior design by Gopa & Ted2, Inc.

Printed in the United States of America
Distributed by Publishers Group West

10 9 8 7 6 5 4 3 2 1

For Jerilyn

Contents

# Introduction

"I've had every opportunity and blessing in my own life, and I want the same for all Americans. Until that day comes, you will always find me on the front lines of democracy: fighting for the future."

Hillary Rodham Clinton concedes her bid for the presidency, June 7, 2008

IT's HARD TO BELIEVE that Hillary Clinton has been making headlines for several decades, but once her term as one of the most admired secretaries of state in history drew to a close in 2012, all eyes naturally turned to what her plans would be during the years leading up to the 2016 presidential campaign season.

Representative Nancy Pelosi recently admitted to

MSNBC that she was excited by the prospect of seeing a second Clinton in the Oval Office. "She could be president of the United States and she would be great," Pelosi said. "She would go into the White House as well prepared . . . or better prepared . . . than almost anybody who has served in that office in a very long time."

Surprisingly, even her most dogged detractors concede that it would be difficult to run against her. "The Republican Party is incapable of competing at that level," said none other than Newt Gingrich during an appearance on NBC's *Meet the Press*. "First of all, she's very formidable as a person," he said. "She's a very competent person. She's married to the most popular Democrat in the country, and they both think [it] would be good for her to be president. It makes it virtually impossible to stop her for the nomination."

She has certainly proven that she has the stamina and fortitude to serve as president: In her tenure as secretary of state, by her own estimation, she traveled to 112 countries, clocking close to a million miles, a schedule that would send most of her Washington cohorts falling by the wayside.

And early public sentiment is overwhelmingly favorable: A December 2012 *Washington Post* poll found that

68 percent of Americans approved of her accomplishments as secretary of state, 66 percent had a favorable opinion of her, and 57 percent would support her as a presidential candidate.

With these figures, it's not surprising that Clinton was named as the most admired woman for the eleventh year in a row in a recent Gallup Poll; in all, she's made the list seventeen times, more than any other woman. Interest in Clinton only continues to climb; plus, she has a cool factor that was only enhanced when the *Texts from Hillary* Tumblr site went viral almost from the first post in spring 2012, showing her in sunglasses on the C-17 military plane she customarily traveled on and texting on her BlackBerry.

No less than Hollywood has taken notice: *Rodham*, a much-buzzed-about screenplay that is gaining traction, covers Clinton's formidable twenty-something years and is rumored to be on the fast track for green-lighting; actresses rumored to be clamoring for the lead include Emma Stone, Ellen Page, and Lena Dunham.

But Hillary is more than just politics; after all, she's held numerous important leadership positions in her career, from high-powered lawyer to two-term First Lady, in addition to being a respected senator and secretary of state.

Plus, she's been through more than a few rough-and-tumble periods in her life; indeed, many men and women around the world have followed her as she's been knocked down through the years only to pick herself right up again.

In this way, *Hillary Clinton in Her Own Words* accomplishes several purposes, regardless of what her plans for 2016 turn out to be. First, the book will appeal to politically minded readers who can learn where she's stood on a wide variety of issues over the years; it will serve as a refresher course for those who have followed her life over the decades she's spent in public life as well as provide an introduction for younger readers who may be acquainted with the former First Lady only as a world diplomat.

Next, her words will educate businesspeople who want to learn about her philosophies on leadership. After all, her roaring success as secretary of state was due in no small part to her ability to negotiate and communicate with world leaders often holding very different agendas.

Finally, Clinton's words will motivate and inspire people around the world who look to her as an example of the courage and fortitude they can source in their own lives.

Regardless of your reason for picking up *Hillary Clinton in Her Own Words*, after reading her words on everything from motherhood to the role of government, you will undoubtedly come away with a new understanding and broader picture of the woman who just may become the next president of the United States.

Timeline

1947: Hillary Rodham is born in Chicago to Hugh and Dorothy Rodham on October 26.

1961: Fourteen-year-old Hillary writes a letter to NASA asking what she should study in college in order to become an astronaut. The letter she receives in response informs her that women cannot become astronauts.

1964: Hillary signs on as a volunteer in the presidential campaign of Barry Goldwater, a Republican.

1965: She enrolls at Wellesley College.

1969: Hillary graduates from Wellesley College, where she becomes the first student in the school's history to give the commencement speech. She enrolls at Yale Law School in the fall.

1970: While at Yale Law School, she meets fellow student Bill Clinton.

1973: Hillary graduates from Yale Law School.

1974: In January, Hillary moves to Washington, DC, to become a member of the congressional legal staff involved in preparing the case for impeachment against President Richard Nixon. In August, Hillary accepts a job at the University of Arkansas School of Law in Fayetteville, in part to be closer to Bill.

1975: Hillary and Bill marry on October 10.

1976: After Bill is elected attorney general of Arkansas, Hillary lands a job at Rose Law Firm and they move to Little Rock.

1979: Bill begins his first term as governor of Arkansas, and Hillary becomes First Lady of the state.

1980: Daughter Chelsea is born on February 27. Hillary is named partner at Rose Law Firm.

1992: Bill is elected president of the United States, and Hillary becomes First Lady.

1996: Hillary's first book, *It Takes a Village*, is published.

2000: Hillary and Bill leave the White House after two full terms of his presidency and move to Chappaqua, New York. Hillary launches her campaign to become the junior senator from New York and wins the election with 53 percent of the vote. She is the first First Lady ever to win elective office.

2001: Hillary begins her first term in the Senate.

2003: Hillary's second book, *Living History*, is published.

2006: Hillary runs for her second term as senator and is reelected with a whopping 67 percent of the vote.

2007: On January 20—exactly two years before the next Inauguration Day—Hillary announces she is running for president.

2008: On January 8, Hillary wins the all-important New Hampshire primary. On June 7, she announces she is ending her quest for the Democratic nomination. On December 1, President-elect Obama appoints Hillary to serve as his secretary of state.

2009–2012: Hillary runs a nonstop program of international diplomacy, crisscrossing the globe to meet with the presidents and rulers of 112 countries, racking up almost a million miles in the process.

2012: Hillary steps down from her position as secretary of state after Obama's first term ends.

Quotations

⊰≫ Abortion

I am and always have been pro-choice, and . . . it is not a right that any of us should take for granted. There are a number of forces at work in our society that would try to turn back the clock and undermine a woman's right to choose, and we must remain vigilant.

The New York Times, January 22, 2000

I've been saying the same thing for as long as I can remember: I believe abortion should be safe, legal, and rare. I do think women should have a choice but also that women should be making responsible decisions. I think people who have been pro-choice have basically gotten lazy about [being politically active].

Marie Claire, August 24, 2007

Forces are aligned to change this country and strip away the rights we enjoy and have come to expect. Slowly, methodically, quietly, they have begun chipping away at the reproductive rights of women. And if those rights fall, other rights will follow. Their goal is to supplant modern society with a society that fits into their narrow worldview. It all starts with an assault on *Roe*.

Speech, NARAL, January 22, 2004

I think abortion should remain legal, but it needs to be safe and rare. And I have spent many years now, as a private citizen, as First Lady, and now as senator, trying to make it rare, trying to create the conditions where women had other choices. I have supported adoption and foster care. I helped to create the campaign against teenage pregnancy, which fulfilled our original goal ten years ago of reducing teenage pregnancies by about a third. And I am committed to do even more.

Democratic Candidates Compassion Forum, Messiah College, April 13, 2008

I have met thousands and thousands of pro-choice men and women. I have never met anyone who is pro-abortion. Being pro-choice is not being pro-abortion. Being pro-choice is trusting the individual to make the right decision for herself and her family and not entrusting that decision to anyone wearing the authority of government in any regard.

Speech, NARAL, January 22, 1999

⊰⊱ Age

I feel so relieved to be at the stage I'm at in my life right now, because if I want to wear my glasses, I'm wearing my glasses. If I want to pull my hair back, I'm pulling my hair back. And at some point it's just not something that deserves a whole lot of time and attention, and if others want to worry about it, I'll let them do the worrying for a change.

CNN, May 8, 2012

⊰ Agricultural Policy

We have to have more focus on family farms. We've got to do more to make sure trade agreements are not only good for the exporting of agricultural products from great, big agribusiness, but also for small farmers. We've got to do more to build up the agricultural and rural areas of our country.

Democratic Primary Debate, *This Week with George Stephanopoulos*, August 19, 2007

⊰ America

I believe our values represent the greatest accomplishment in political history and the history of the world, and those values are not just American values. So I believe the United States has both an opportunity and obligation to make clear around the world that democracy and freedom, free market economies that are open, and meritocracies, providing support for people's human rights and those fundamental badges of liberty that we know enhance your God-given potential, that's who we are as a people.

The Today Show, October 12, 2011

We always led with our values, and the idea that, unlike most other leading nations in history in the world, we weren't out to build an empire, we were not out to impose an ideology on the unwilling. We happen to believe that we best represent the full flowering of the human potential, and therefore, we want to exemplify it, we want to stand for it, and we want to lead toward it.

Time, October 27, 2011

We have a system that truly does work, if only we become involved in it.

Hillary Rodham Clinton: A First Lady for Our Time, 1999

⊰⊱ American Leadership

We do have to keep innovating and integrating. We have to get our house here at home in order. We have to avoid devastating self-inflicted wounds. We have to remain committed to upholding America's global leadership and our core values of freedom and opportunity.

Speech, Joint Civilian Service Award Presentation,
February 14, 2013

I think when you inherit the range of problems that we have, from one end of the world to the other—the threats that we faced, the two wars that we inherited—I think trying to have a very clear approach to actually dealing with those problems [and promoting] American leadership at this time in our history is about as big an idea as you can get.

Newsweek, April 22, 2010

⊰ The American Political System

What's great about our political system is that we are all judged on our own merits.

Democratic Primary Debate, Los Angeles, January 31, 2008

⊰ America's Greatest Threat

The greatest threat to us as a nation is that we start looking both inward and backward, and that we begin to doubt ourselves, and that we don't even believe as much in ourselves as others still believe in us.

Time, October 27, 2011

⇥ America's Role in the World

Our country is not only the leader of the world, but we are expected to be by countless nations around the globe. And yes, we have challenges here at home, but these are challenges that we can meet. I'm very confident and optimistic about what America is capable of. I've lived through in my life a lot of ups and downs in our country, but you can never count America out and you should never bet against America.

The Today Show, October 12, 2011

I cannot tell you how many people say things to me like, "Well, we don't always agree with what the Americans do, but we don't think you have ill motives or ill intent. We think sometimes you don't do the right thing." And it's funny because there's that overarching impression that we're not out to build an empire, we're not out to take over these countries, we're not out to enslave them.

Reuters, October 13, 2011

We can't just walk out of the arena and leave these important decisions to somebody else because it's messy, it's difficult, it requires compromise. That is what you have to do on the world stage today. We remain the strongest country in the world, but the way we exercise that leadership has changed dramatically.

Newsweek, April 22, 2010

The United States can't solve all of the problems in the world. But the problems in the world can't be solved without the United States. And therefore, we have to husband our resources, among which is this incredibly valuable asset of global leadership, and figure out how we can best deploy it.

The New York Times Magazine, June 27, 2012

The United States bears a disproportionate amount of the burden for trying to maintain peace and security and prosperity across the globe. I wish there were a way we could tell a lot of countries what they should do.

The Secretary, 2013

❧ Her Appearance

If I want to knock a story off the front page, I just change my hairstyle.

Newsweek, June 4, 1995

Everything I said or did—and even what I wore—became a hot button for debate. Hair and fashion were my first clues. For most of my life I had paid little attention to my clothes. I liked headbands. They were easy, and I couldn't imagine that they suggested anything good, bad or indifferent about me to the American public. But during the campaign, some of my friends began a mission to spruce up my appearance. They brought me racks of clothes to try on, and they told me the headband had to go. What they understood, and I didn't, was that a First Lady's appearance matters. I was no longer representing only myself. I was asking the American people to let me represent them in a role that has conveyed everything from glamour to comfort.

Living History, 2003

⊰⊱ Asia

We do see Asia as part of America's future. We are both a transatlantic and a transpacific power. And part of what I hope we can do is better understand and create the kind of future that will benefit both Asians and Americans.

The Secretary, 2013

⊰⊱ Balancing Your Life

Most of us will at some point get married and have children, and how you balance that really depends on the quality of your friends and whether your friends are there for you. It also depends on what the policies are in your workplace.

Marie Claire, August 24, 2007

The first lesson I've learned is that no matter what you do in your life, you have to figure out your own internal rhythms—I mean, what works for you doesn't necessarily work for your friend. I try to schedule at least one day a week to catch up, to feel like I'm breathing again.

Marie Claire, August 24, 2007

⇥ Becoming a Grandmother

Let me just say I love babies, so maybe I'll have more in my life someday.

Good Morning America, January 18, 2011

⇥ Being Secretary of State

The work that I tried to do was intense and personal because I saw no other way around getting out there, not only interacting with governments but wading into popular culture, people to people, because I also had been absorbing data about what just average people thought about the United States. . . . So it was a great effort to get back out there.

The Economist, March 22, 2012

It's never the same, literally from hour to hour, which is why the job is so exciting for me.

The Today Show, October 12, 2011

What I have found hardest to balance is the amount of travel that is expected today. One would think that in an era where communication is instantaneous, you would not have to get on an airplane and go sit in a meeting. But, in fact, it's almost as though people are more desirous of seeing someone in person.

Newsweek, December 20, 2009

One of my goals upon becoming Secretary of State was to take diplomacy out of capitals, out of government offices, into the media, into the streets of countries. So from the very beginning in February of 2009, I have tried to combine the necessary diplomacy of government meetings, of creating structures in which we enhance our participation government-to-government with people-to-people diplomacy.

Time, October 27, 2011

Part of my mission has been to make it clear that American leadership was back. What I found when I became Secretary of State was a lot of doubts and a lot of concerns and fears from friends, allies, around the world. And so part of what I have tried to do as Secretary of State is to reassert American leadership, but to recognize that in twenty-first century terms we have to lead differently than the way we historically have done.

Time, October 27, 2011

There might be times when our criticism is private and other times when it's public, when it's a one-off, and other times when it's persistent—because you're always trying to calibrate what will work. I mean, I'm not into just criticizing for the sake of criticizing. You're trying to give voice to and support to people who are standing up for values that are important.

PBS Newshour with Jim Lehrer, December 14, 2011

It's an impossible job, because in the world we live in, it is 24/7, there is no respite. . . . I would like to say okay, I think I'll just concentrate on the Middle East, on our relations with China, on the reset with Russia. Okay, well then what about everybody else and everything that they're doing, and the importance of other countries, other regions, to our future? For example, Latin America is one of the most important regions to America's future. We have more trade with our friends in Latin America than anywhere else in the world. We have democratic values in common with the vast majority of countries. So we can't afford to say okay, well fine, we're not going to be engaged in and working on these issues. We have to be open to being a part of making the world better everywhere. And that is a big challenge.

The Today Show, October 12, 2011

⊰ Being True to Herself

You have to be true to yourself. You have to be enough in touch with who you are and what you want, how you want to live and what's important to you, to make your decisions based on that. Sometimes that's very difficult. Sometimes it's hard to have your own internal voice be heard . . . it's hard because you've got society with expectations and you've got family, friends, and others who are expressing opinions. When you're in the public eye, it's like open season with the entire world. You have just one life to live. It is yours. Own it, claim it, live it, do the best you can with it.

Marie Claire, October 18, 2012

⊰ The Bible

If I quote a Bible Scripture, people are always looking for the hidden meaning in it.

Newsweek, October 30, 1994

Ever since I was a little girl, I have been a great admirer of Esther. I used to ask that that story be read to me over and over again, because there weren't too many models of women who had the opportunity to make a decision that was very courageous. Esther is someone who I wish I knew even more about than what we know from the Bible.

Democratic Compassion Forum, Messiah College, April 13, 2008

Matthew 5, 6 and 7. Those three chapters I think are just filled with challenge and it's very hard to read and for me to fully understand. Or the whole Book of James—because I, being a Methodist, am big on deeds as well as words.

Newsweek, October 30, 1994

⤳ Bill Clinton as a Father

[Bill] was amazed by fatherhood. He was overwhelmed by it. I've heard him say that when he saw his child, he realized it was more than his own father got to do.

[Clinton's natural father died before he was born.] And he has worked very hard and has been a real supportive father.

Newsweek, February 2, 1992

⋈ Bill Clinton as First Husband

He will not have a formal official role. But just as presidents rely on wives, husbands, fathers, friends of long years, he will be my close confidant and adviser, as I was with him. I doubt that there will be an important issue that I won't talk to him about. I don't think there was an important issue that he didn't talk to me about. I don't talk about everything we talked about, because obviously I don't think that's appropriate. But I expect to rely on him in a personal way, and I expect to ask him to take on some very important assignments.

This Week with George Stephanopoulos, December 30, 2007

⊰⊱ Bipartisanship in Washington

Too often in Washington today, reaching across the aisle seems as controversial as negotiating with the Taliban. That is not the way democracy is supposed to work.

Huffington Post, June 26, 2013

Whether you're on the right or the left, you cannot believe you have the only truth. That's not the way a democracy works. That's not the way our country has succeeded. You have to listen to each other, and yes, you have to find compromise.

The Today Show, October 12, 2011

You've got to get Republicans and Democrats together. That's what I will do.

Democratic Primary Debate, Philadelphia, April 16, 2008

⇥ Building Relationships with Other Countries

I think it's important not just to go once and kind of wave and have the meetings and not return, but to build those relationships and to look for ways that we can not just have the United States present, but in a position to help manage some of the upcoming problems that we know are just over the horizon.

The Today Show, October 12, 2011

⇥ Campaign Finance Reform

We need public financing, a total overhaul of how we fund our campaigns.

This Week with George Stephanopoulos, December 30, 2007

I'm very much in favor of public financing, which is the only way to really change a lot of the problems that we have in our campaign finance system . . . [which] is a problem for every campaign. I have more than 100,000 donors, the vast majority of whom have given me less than $100. We're spending an enormous amount of time and effort raising money, mostly to be clear to go on television. It is not good for our political system. There has to be a way that public financing becomes the law.

Meet the Press, September 23, 2007

There is this artificial distinction that people are trying to make: Don't take money from lobbyists, but take money from the people who employ and hire lobbyists and give them their marching orders. . . . I think we can do a much better job if we say we have got to move toward public financing, get the money out of American politics, because it's the people who employ the lobbyists who are behind all the money in American politics.

Democratic Primary Debate, *This Week with George Stephanopoulos*, August 19, 2007

⇥ Her Chances to Win the Presidency

I believe that both my theory and my strategy, and my track record and how I'm doing right now, really adds up to a very compelling argument that I will actually win.

Boston Globe, October 11, 2007

⇥ Chef Alice Waters

I think she's been a breakthrough figure in American cuisine, in the kind of food she's prepared and in the kind of positions she's taken. I think what she says makes a lot of sense.

The New York Times, February 2, 1993

⊰≫ Her Childhood

When I was a little younger . . . I thought I wanted to be an astronaut and I wrote off to NASA and they wrote back saying, you know, we're not taking girls.

ABC News, June 8, 2003

I never felt anything but support from my family. Whatever I thought I could do and be, they supported. There was no distinction between me and my brothers or any barriers thrown up to me that I couldn't think about something because I was a girl. If you work hard enough and you really apply yourself then you should be able to do whatever you choose to do.

Hillary Rodham Clinton: A First Lady for Our Time, 1993

⊰≫ Children

We cannot permit discussions of children and families to be subverted by political or ideological debate. There are strong feelings about what should or should not be done, but there are also, I believe, strong areas of agreement where people should get beyond their disagreements to work together. There should be no disagreement about the fact that the family structure is in trouble not only here, but in many parts of the world. There should be no debate that children need the nurturing and care that a stable family can provide.

Speech, United Methodist General Conference, April 24, 1996

⚛ China

We will continue to raise [the issue of human rights] and we will listen to our Chinese partners' responses. We will encourage progress in this area. And we think it's very valuable to make sure that the relationship is strong and stable so that when we have areas of disagreement, which we certainly will have, that we continue our talking and our working together despite that.

Interview with Caixin Media Company, May 11, 2011

We don't walk away from dealing with China because we think they have a deplorable human rights record. . . . They're worried, and they are trying to stop history, which is a fool's errand. They cannot do it. But they're going to hold it off as long as possible.

The Atlantic, May 10, 2011

China . . . [is] still, by any standard, a poor country. And yes, there are great pockets of wealth and success, but that isn't reflected in the overall standard of living, and our national wealth is so much greater, many times over, than China's. So let's put this into some perspective about what's actually real and what is feared or a source of anxiety.

Interview with Reuters, October 11, 2011

We are two different nations based on history and experience and perspective, so we are not going to see the world the same way, we're not going to agree on everything. That would make it very boring, I believe. So what we best can do is honestly express our opinions. Nothing is off the table, nothing is hidden; everything is to be presented and discussed. And that's what we've been doing.

Interview with Caixin Media Company, May 11, 2011

⊰ᴷ Her Communication Style

With every tough message that I deliver, it is embedded in a much broader context. It's not, "You're with us or against us." It is, "We have a lot of business to do."

Newsweek, April 22, 2010

⊰ᴷ Communism

We would always be engaged in a struggle with Communism—that would determine our entire lives. That was pounded into us [as children]. That was the worldview we were given.

Hillary Rodham Clinton: A First Lady for Our Time, 1993

❧ Community

Why is it in a country as economically wealthy as we are despite our economic problems, in a country that is the longest-surviving democracy, there is this undercurrent of discontent—this sense that somehow economic growth and prosperity, political democracy and freedom are not enough? That we lack, at some core level, meaning in our individual lives and meaning collectively—that sense that our lives are part of some greater effort, that we are connected to one another, that community means that we have a place where we belong no matter who we are?

Speech, University of Texas at Austin, April 7, 1993

❧ Corporate America

Corporate America today doesn't see middle class and working Americans. They are invisible. They don't understand that if you're a family that can't get health care, you are really hurting. But to the corporate elite . . . you're invisible. . . . So I think we need to get both public sector and private sector leadership to start stepping up and being responsible and taking care of people.

Democratic Primary Debate, South Carolina, April 26, 2007

⊰ Crime

We have to do all of these things. . . . We do have to go after racial profiling. I've supported legislation to try to tackle that. . . . We have to go after mandatory minimums. You know, mandatory sentences for certain violent crimes may be appropriate, but it has been too widely used. And it now has a discriminatory impact. . . . We need diversion, like drug courts. Non-violent offenders should not be serving hard time in our prisons. They need to be diverted from our prison system.

Democratic Primary Debate, Howard University, June 28, 2007

We will never build enough prisons to end our crime problem.

SFGate, February 7, 1996

⚘ Her Critics

If I worried about every time anybody said something nasty about me . . . I would be incapacitated.

Midwest Today, June 1994

Why would they spend their time . . . going after me and misrepresenting things that I had said and worked on? And then I said to myself, "Well, obviously they're scared." You don't spend two or three days at a national political convention beating up on someone unless you're scared.

Hillary Rodham Clinton: A First Lady for Our Time, 1993

I was amused when one commentator wrote that my critics were divided between conservatives who suspect I did not mean what I said and liberals who feared that I did.

Speech, National Prayer Luncheon, February 2, 1994

It would be hard to find anybody who has incurred the wrath of the special interests more than I have: the drug companies, the health-insurance companies, the oil companies. You just go down the list.

This Week with George Stephanopoulos, December 29, 2007

You always get angry when people lie about you, but it doesn't do very much good to just stay angry because it saps up too much of your energy. You have to do the very best you can every day to give people a chance to get to know you, and to try to refute the things that are said about you. And that's all you can do.

Hillary Rodham Clinton: A First Lady for Our Time, 1993

I learned a long time ago, because my husband has been in this business for so long, that unfair criticism goes with the territory. And for me the challenge has been to take criticism seriously but not personally. I mean, if somebody has something legitimate to say that is grounded in fact, I'm interested in it. If they have their own opinion about who I am or what I should be, I'm really not that interested in it because that's their opinion, and there's a million of them. And there's just no time to spend worrying about people who say mean things about you.

Midwest Today, June 1994

⊰ Daily Life

From my perspective, you get up every day and you get out there and you make your case, and you reach as many people as possible.

This Week with George Stephanopoulos, December 29, 2007

I just take it a day at a time—it's a good policy for life as well as politics.

Vanity Fair, August 2008

⇥ Her Daughter

I am just bursting with maternal pride over [Chelsea], who I look to also for advice and, frankly, for some cultural cues that I might otherwise miss.

Official Swearing-In Ceremony as Secretary of State, February 2, 2009

I think she does have the public service bug. That seems to be in our DNA. I think she wants to help make a difference and she wants to use the experiences and opportunities she's been given during the course of her life to figure out what her own contribution will be.

The Today Show, October 12, 2011

I have tried very hard to put my obligation to my daughter ahead of everything. And one of the things I have tried to do is make sure she not only had the support she needed but the time she needed. You never know in retrospect whether you did or didn't do exactly the right thing—stay-at-home mothers, gone-away mothers, all of us worry whether we should have done something differently than we did. One of the things that I have given up completely is time with friends and social time. We talk on the phone or try to see each other on special occasions. But I couldn't keep an active social life and do everything else.

Newsweek, February 2, 1992

⇥ The Democratic Party

The Democratic Party is a family. And now it's time to restore the ties that bind us together and to come together around the ideals we share, the values we cherish, and the country we love.

Concession Speech, June 7, 2008

Time and time again, I've helped shape the policy, I've helped advocate for the policy, I've helped defend the policy, and I feel very comfortable where I am in the Democratic Party. I want to get more Democrats elected, so I don't take on my party just for the sake of taking it on. I often try to mold my party and move it so we can agree.

... I think, right now, the Democratic Party is much more in step [than the Republicans].

Politico, February 11, 2008

❧ The District of Columbia

I want to get full voting rights for DC. I think it is an injustice that has to be remedied. I want to be a better partner in working with the district on everything from its transportation challenges to its health care problems.

Politico, February 11, 2008

❧ The Economy

Some think that the market can do anything if left alone. Others undermine the benefits that free enterprise brings. We have to create a balance. How do we enjoy the benefits without suffering from the excesses? The economy can create the jobs ... and wealth. It can create consumers and the producers of goods. But the economy cannot create citizens. Government can only respond to citizens, not create them. Only civil society can do that. And it is time for us to renew and expand civil society.

Speech, The Sorbonne, Paris, June 17, 1999

I believe that the foundation of a strong economy doesn't begin with giving people who are already privileged and wealthy even more benefits. I think it comes from shared prosperity.

Take Back America Conference, June 20, 2007

I will turn this economy around. We will get back to shared prosperity and we will see once again that we can do this the right way so it's not just a government of the few, by the few and for the few.

Democratic Primary Debate, Philadelphia, April 16, 2008

⇴ Education

I'm a strong supporter of early childhood education and universal pre-kindergarten. . . . I'm against No Child Left Behind as it is currently operating. And I would end it, because we can do so much better to have an education system that really focuses in on kids who need extra help.

Democratic Primary Debate, Philadelphia, April 16, 2008

We also know that to be educated, the goal of it must be human liberation. A liberation enabling each of us to fulfill our capacity so as to be free to create within and around ourselves.

Student Commencement Speech, Wellesley College, May 31, 1969

I support school-based merit pay. . . . We need to get more teachers to go into . . . underserved urban areas, underserved rural areas. But the school is a team, and I think it's important that we reward that collaboration. A child who moves from kindergarten to sixth grade in the same school, every one of those teachers is going to affect that child. . . . You need to weed out the teachers who are not doing a good job. That's the bottom line. They should not be teaching our children.

Democratic Primary Debate, Las Vegas, November 15, 2007

I know there are some who believe that vouchers are the way to improve our public schools; I believe they are dead wrong. There is simply no evidence that vouchers improve student achievement. We've been experimenting with vouchers in some jurisdictions . . . for a couple of years, [and] we've found no evidence . . . that these have made any difference in student achievement. But what they have done is to divert much-needed public funds for the few and have weakened the entire system.

Speech, National Education Association, Orlando, July 5, 1999

I think teachers are professionals and should be treated as professionals. That's why I believe that we should test teachers in the beginning to make sure that when they got their teaching degree, that they're qualified.

New York Senate Debate, October 28, 2000

What we're trying to do is change the culture within schools and to provide the resources, the training, and the support that teachers need to do the job they do want to do. . . . You have to reform No Child Left Behind. We're going to try to do that and begin to make it much more in line with the reality of teaching.

Democratic Primary Debate, *This Week with George Stephanopoulos*, August 19, 2007

I don't think [merit pay is] a very good way to inspire teachers. We want our best teachers to work with the kids who are the hardest to teach. If teachers are going to be told that the people who look better on a test are the ones who are going to get them rewarded in salary or compensation, why would anyone take on the kids who are harder to teach?

The New York Times, April 6, 2000

⊰꧇ The Education of Women

Educating young women is not only morally right, but it is also the most important investment any society can make in order to further and advance the values and the interests of the people.

The Secretary, 2013

⊰꧇ Empowerment

I've spent a lifetime trying to empower people, trying to fight for them.

Democratic Primary Debate, Philadelphia, April 16, 2008

⊰꧇ Energy Policy

If we have [$4/gallon gas], then we should have a windfall profits tax on these outrageous profits of the oil companies, and put that money back into the highway trust fund, so that we don't lose out on repair and construction and rebuilding.

Democratic Primary Debate, Philadelphia, April 16, 2008

⊁ English as "Official" Language

It is important that English remain our common unifying language because that brings our country together in a way that we have seen generations of immigrants coming to our shores be able to be part of the American experience and pursue the American dream. I have been adamantly against the efforts by some to make English the official language. That I do not believe is appropriate, and I have voted against it and spoken against it. I represent New York. We have 170 languages in NYC alone. I do not think we should be, in any way, discriminating against people who do not speak English, who use facilities like hospitals or have to go to court to enforce their rights. But English does remain an important part of the American experience.

Democratic Primary Debate, University of Texas at Austin, February 21, 2008

⇥ Equal Pay

Equal pay is not yet equal. A woman makes 77 cents on a dollar and women of color make 67 cents. . . . We feel so passionately about this because we not only are running for office, but we each, in our own way, have lived it. We have seen it. We have understood the pain and the injustice that has come because of race, because of gender. And it's imperative that . . . we make it very clear that each of us will address these issues.

Democratic Primary Debate, Congressional Black Caucus Institute, January 21, 2008

⇥ Evil

There are evil people in the world. And they may be able to come up with elaborate rationalizations to attempt to explain their evil, and they may even have some reasonable basis for saying their conduct needs to be understood in the light of pre-existing conditions, but their behavior is still evil.

The New York Times Magazine, May 23, 1993

⊰⊱ Facing Challenges

You know, in life you get knocked down from time to time. Sometimes you don't know it's coming.

Vanity Fair, August 2008

The most difficult decisions I have made in my life were to stay married to Bill and to run for the Senate from New York.

Living History, 2003

⊰⊱ Faith

I am an old-fashioned Methodist.

Newsweek, October 30, 1994

I was raised with faith, and that's a great gift to give a child, and I have relied on it. I've relied on prayer. I had to reach deep down into my own faith and ask myself, what is it that I thought was right to do? And there were many people who were giving me all kinds of conflicting advice, and I appreciated their interest and their support, but ultimately I had to get on my knees and I had to pray and I had to look for answers that only could come to me. You have to decide to do what you think is right, because your friends won't be there at 3:00 in the morning.

ABC News, June 8, 2003

You have to fight this feeling of hopelessness and help-lessness in your own life as well as in the lives of people around you. I'm blessed with the kind of religious faith and upbringing that has given me a lot that I can fall back on.

Live with Regis and Kathie Lee, June 10, 1996

We know that acting on our faith is never easy. And it is often a test of our own resolve as much as anything else.

Speech, United Methodist General Conference, April 24, 1996

Faith is something I take very seriously. I do not believe I am a very good Christian. I think it is extremely hard to be a Christian. I think every day is a challenge to one's Christianity, and that by growing in faith, minute by minute, hour by hour, faith becomes stronger and deeper and bigger and opens one's eyes to greater possibilities and further challenges.

Speech, National Prayer Luncheon, February 2, 1994

In the world in which I'm living now, there is so much emphasis on the short term and the secular, I feel really grateful to have some sense of faith and rooting that goes beyond that. And to be reminded that you have to try to stand for something bigger than yourself.

Hillary Rodham Clinton: A First Lady for Our Time, 1993

⚛ Her Father

My dad, Hugh Rodham, was a rock-ribbed, up-by-your-bootstraps, conservative Republican and proud of it. He was also tight-fisted with money. He did not believe in credit and he ran his business on a strict pay-as-you-go policy. His ideology was based on self-reliance and personal initiative, but unlike many people who call themselves conservatives today, he understood the importance of fiscal responsibility and supported taxpayer investments in highways, schools, parks, and other important public goods. My father could not stand waste. Like so many who grew up in the Depression, his fear of poverty colored his life. To this day, I put uneaten olives back in the jar, wrap up the tiniest pieces of cheese, and feel guilty when I throw anything away.

Living History, 2003

⊰⊱ Feminism

I am a woman and, like millions of women, I know there are still barriers and biases out there, often unconscious, and I want to build an America that respects and embraces the potential of every last one of us.

Concession Speech, June 7, 2008

⊰ᚻ Fighting

You show people what you're willing to fight for when you fight your friends.

Cabinet and Staff Retreat at Camp David, January 1993

The harder they hit, the more encouraged I get.

The Unique Voice of Hillary Rodham Clinton, 1996

⊰ᚻ Being First Lady

There's nothing comparable to being First Lady. It's not a job; it's a role or a position. It is remade every time someone fills it, because of the election, up until now, of a husband as President. . . . It was a hard adjustment for me.

The New Yorker, October 13, 2003

I know that no matter what I did—if I did nothing, if I spent my entire day totally disengaged from what was going on around me—I'd be criticized for that. I mean, it's a no-win deal, no matter what I do, or try to do.

The New York Times Magazine, May 23, 1993

⊰⊱ Foreign Aid

In Congress, there are some who ... think ... if we just cut [foreign aid], we'd be able to balance the budget. And so we've been doing a lot of educating with our colleagues on the Hill to make the case: Look, this is a historic moment with so much that is happening. . . . We have to be opening markets, creating more investment. There's just a big agenda out there.

Interview with Reuters, October 13, 2011

⊰⊱ Foreign Policy

There will be times when not all of our interests align. We work to align them, but that is just reality.

The Secretary, 2013

We now understand that America, as powerful and strong as we are, cannot remake societies. We can help liberate them, like Libya, but we cannot remake them. That must come from within . . . and there needs to be higher expectations and demands placed on leaders who should be reconcilers, not dividers.

The Secretary, 2013

What was possible for autocrats and dictators in the past, no longer is. You have to be conscious of what is bubbling below. And so for me, it's this top-down, bottom-up combination, because if people have a good feeling about or understanding of who we are as Americans, that influences what a leader who is inclined to work with us is able to do, and it also sends a message to those who are not.

Time, October 27, 2011

⊰⊱ Forgiveness

[The gift of forgiveness] is one I have needed on a daily basis. . . . Forgiveness is the most powerful expression of love we can give or experience. It is also the most costly. For the Lord, it was the cross; for me, it cost my pride. Forgiving is hard. Forgiving those who seem determined to destroy, to tear down, those who seem to have a political or financial or personal agenda; forgiving those who bear false witness, who delight in spreading stories, gossip, rumor.

Speech, National Prayer Luncheon, February 2, 1994

ᐳᐱ Free Trade

We've got to have a better approach . . . to trade around the world. And it's important that we have an idea of how to maximize the benefits from the global economy while minimizing the impact on American workers. That includes things like real trade adjustment assistance and other support.

AFL-CIO Democratic Primary Forum, August 8, 2007

Trade needs to become a win-win. People ask me, am I a free trader or a fair trader? I want to be a smart, pro-American trader. And that means we look for ways to maximize the impact of what we're trying to export and quit being taken advantage of by other countries.

Democratic Primary Debate, *This Week with George Stephanopoulos*, August 19, 2007

⊱ Freedom

Americans believe that the desire for dignity and self-determination is universal, and we do try to act on that belief around the world. Americans have fought and died for these ideals. And when freedom gains ground anywhere, Americans are inspired.

The Secretary, 2013

⊱ The Future

The kind of help we need in the twenty-first century is for people themselves to overcome the differences that still divide them.

The Secretary, 2013

⊰ Gay Rights and Marriage

Being gay is not a Western invention; it is a human reality.

Speech, International Human Rights Day, Geneva,
Switzerland, December 6, 2011

Gay rights are human rights.

Speech, International Human Rights Day, Geneva,
Switzerland, December 6, 2011

I support it personally and as a matter of policy and law. Marriage is a fundamental building block of our society—a great joy and, yes, a great responsibility. To deny the opportunity to any of our daughters and sons solely on the basis of who they are and who they love is to deny them the chance to live up to their own God-given abilities.

Speech, Human Rights Campaign Video, March 18, 2013

⊰ God

I think God is omnipotent and omniscient. I think that because of the fact that I am a child of my tradition and have developed as I have over time, I think of God more in a Father sense. But that's not exclusive to me. I don't discount characteristics and virtues of the feminine by saying and thinking that. But that is the tradition I grew up in and it is accessible to me, so I'm more likely to rely on it.

Newsweek, October 30, 1994

I have, ever since I've been a little girl, felt the presence of God in my life. And it has been a gift of grace that has, for me, been incredibly sustaining. . . . I have had experiences on many, many occasions where I felt like the Holy Spirit was there with me as I made a journey. It didn't have to be a hard time. It could be taking a walk in the woods. It could be watching a sunset. . . . I don't think that I could have made my life's journey without being anchored in God's grace and without having that sense of forgiveness and unconditional love. . . . My faith has given me the confidence to make decisions that were right for me, whether anybody else agreed with me or not.

Democratic Candidates Compassion Forum, Messiah College, April 13, 2008

❧ Government Cronyism

Let's start by cleaning up the government, replacing this culture of corruption and cronyism with a culture of competence and caring again. Let's stop outsourcing critical government functions to private companies that overcharge and underperform! Let's close the revolving door between government and the lobbying shop, and let's end the no-bid contracts for Halliburton and the other well-connected companies!

Take Back America Conference, June 20, 2007

How about the radical idea of appointing people who are actually qualified for the positions that we ask them to hold for us? Well, when I'm president, the entrance to the White House will no longer be a revolving door for the well connected, but a door of opportunity for the well qualified.

Take Back America Conference, June 20, 2007

⊰⊱ Government Surveillance versus the Right to Privacy

Unchecked mass surveillance without judicial review may sometimes be legal but it is dangerous. Every president should save those powers for limited critical situations.

Associated Press, June 16, 2006

⊰⊱ Government Transparency

I want to have a much more transparent government, and I think we now have the tools to make that happen. . . . I want to have as much information about the way our government operates on the Internet so the people who pay for it, the taxpayers of America, can see that. . . .

I want people in all the government agencies to be communicating with people, because for me, we're now in an era—which didn't exist before—where you can have instant access to information, and I want to see my government be more transparent.

Meet the Press, January 13, 2008

⊰⊱ The Government's Role in Family

No government can love a child, and no policy can substitute for a family's care. But at the same time, government can either support or undermine families as they cope with the moral, social and economic stresses of caring for children.

Speech, Child Welfare League, March 1, 1995

⊰ Her Guilty Pleasure

When I get tired of reading hundreds and hundreds of pages of depressing reports about what's happening somewhere or another, I either watch decorating shows on television or I read what we call shelter magazines that tell you how to decorate your home if you have the time to do so.

Speech, Conference on "Power: Women as Drivers of Growth and Social Inclusion," Lima, Peru, October 16, 2012

⊰ Gun Control

I respect the Second Amendment. I respect the rights of lawful gun owners to own guns, to use their guns, but I also believe that most lawful gun owners whom I have spoken with for many years across our country also want to be sure that we keep those guns out of the wrong hands. And as president, I will work to try to bridge this divide, which I think has been polarizing and, frankly, doesn't reflect the common sense of the American people. We will strike the right balance to protect the constitutional right but to give people the feeling and the reality that they will be protected from guns in the wrong hands.

Democratic Primary Debate, Philadelphia, April 16, 2008

If you own a gun, make sure it's locked up and stored without the ammunition. In fact, make sure it's stored where the ammunition is stored separately. We've made some progress in the last several years with the Brady Bill and some of the bans on assault weapons, but we have a lot of work to do.

Good Morning America, June 4, 1999

We have to do everything possible to keep guns out of the hands of children, and we need to stand firm on behalf of sensible gun control legislation. . . . It does not make sense for us at this point in our history to turn our backs on the reality that there are too many guns and too many children have access to those guns—and we have to act to prevent that.

Speech, National Education Association, Orlando, Florida, July 5, 1999

I am against illegal guns, and illegal guns are the cause of so much death and injury in our country. I also am a political realist and I understand that the political winds are very powerful against doing enough to try to get guns off the street, get them out of the hands of young people. . . . I don't want the federal government preempting states and cities like New York that have very specific problems. . . . We need to have a registry that really works with good information about people who are felons, people who have been committed to mental institutions. . . . I would also work to reinstate the assault weapons ban. We now have, once again, police deaths going up around the country, and in large measure because bad guys now have assault weapons again.

Democratic Primary Debate, Las Vegas, January 15, 2008

⊰⧽ Her Health

I am, thankfully, knock on wood, not only healthy, but have incredible stamina and energy.

ABC News, December 12, 2012

⇥ How People Perceive Her

Sometimes it is hard even for me to recognize the Hillary Clinton that other people see.

Creators Syndicate, August 1, 2001

I'm a Rorschach test.

Esquire, August 1993

It seemed that people could perceive me only as one thing or the other—EITHER a professional woman OR a conscientious hostess. Gender stereotypes trap women by categorizing them in ways that don't reflect the true complexities of their lives. It was becoming clear to me that people who wanted me to fit into a certain box, traditionalist or feminist, would never be entirely satisfied with me as me—which is to say, with my many different, and sometimes paradoxical roles. In my own mind, I was traditional in some ways and not in others. I cared about the food I served our guests, and I also wanted to improve the delivery of health care for all Americans. To me, there was nothing incongruous about my interests and activities.

Living History, 2003

⊱ How She Does Her Job

I would not be doing my job if I were not looking at the complexity.

The Secretary, 2013

At the end of the day, have you solved the problem or haven't you? Have you crossed it off the list or haven't you?

Newsweek, April 22, 2010

I think I understand not just the headlines . . . but [also] the trend lines. Where is the world going economically? How do we inject economic issues into diplomacy? . . . How do we continue working on big issues like nonproliferation, even though it may not be in the headlines?

So I try to keep a kind of dual track going at all times. What are the immediate, urgent, even emergency issues that I have to deal with, but I don't want to forget what's going to matter to you and my daughter next year, five years, ten years? . . . So it's a real honor but it's also a real challenge and one that I take to my heart because I feel so strongly that America has to lead and America's leadership is absolutely indispensable.

The Today Show, October 12, 2011

⇥ How She Views America

I would ask that people look at us the way I look at us. . . . Name any other society or nation that has done more to help lead the world toward the pursuit of happiness for every individual, for human freedom and dignity, but which, like all human enterprises, is flawed.

The Secretary, 2013

I see America as predominantly a force for good over the course of our history. But I'm also well aware of our flaws and shortcomings, of bad decisions, of misjudgments. We started off as a country that inspired more love of freedom and more opportunity for more people than any other human enterprise in the history of the world, but we still had slaves and we didn't let women vote. So in our own history, there is a continuing striving for that more perfect union.

The Secretary, 2013

⊰ How She Views Herself

I'm smart. I know where I stand on the issues. And I'm not going to change.

Hillary Rodham Clinton: A First Lady for Our Time, 1993

⊰⊱ Her Husband

I am so grateful to him for a lifetime of *all kinds of experiences.*

Official Swearing-In Ceremony as Secretary of State, February 2, 2009

What he's really done for me is share his heart, which is enormous. He is an incredibly loving and compassionate and caring person. And it has made me a better person. He has the most extraordinary amount of patience and love for people of all kinds, and it is almost unfailing. I have watched that ever since I first met him and marveled at it. It has been a standard by which I have judged my own ability to reach out and care and grow.

Midwest Today, June 1994

To this day, [Bill] can astonish me with the connections he weaves between ideas and words and how he makes it all sound like music. I still love the way he thinks and the way he looks.

Living History, 2003

He's also genuinely optimistic and enthusiastic about life. He cares about every day—he wants to jam-pack it with more than the day can hold. It's maddening to try to keep him on any kind of schedule because he wants to listen to everybody. It's not that he doesn't want to go on to the next event; it's just that he doesn't want to leave where he is until he's had a chance to see everybody there.

Midwest Today, June 1994

No one understands me better and no one can make me laugh the way Bill does. Even after all these years, he is still the most interesting, energizing and fully alive person I have ever met.

Living History, 2003

I'm very lucky because my husband is my best friend, and he and I have been together for a very long time, longer than most of you have been alive. We are, we have an endless conversation. We never get bored. We get deeply involved in all of the work that we do, and we talk about it constantly.

The Secretary, 2013

⊰ Her Husband's Political Accomplishments

I'm very proud of my husband's administration. There were a lot of good things that happened, and those good things really changed people's lives. The trajectory of change during those eight years went from deficits and debt to a balanced budget and a surplus, all those 22 million new jobs and the hopefulness that people brought with them. It did take a Clinton to clean after the first Bush, and it might take another one to clean up after the second Bush.

Democratic Primary Debate, Los Angeles, January 31, 2008

⊰ Her Husband's Role in Her Presidency

There are two roles that are really important, and one of them is a historic role that family members of presidents have always played. I've experienced it myself. . . . Somebody who can be a sounding board, who is totally there for you. You don't always agree with what they say, but they can often say . . . why did you do this? Or, maybe you should try that. I will look to him . . . to provide that kind of counsel. At the end of the day, I know better than anyone that the president has to make the decisions. . . . There will be no doubt who wears the pantsuit in my White House.

Politico, February 11, 2008

He'll play a very important role in representing our country around the world. But at the end of the day . . . the weight of decision-making falls on the president. I'm ready to accept that responsibility. I don't believe in government by advisers.

Fox News Sunday with Chris Wallace, February 3, 2008

⇥| Immigration Policy

As president, I would work with our neighbors to the south, to help them create more jobs for their own people. We need to bring the immigrants out of the shadows, give them the conditions that we expect them to meet, paying a fine for coming here illegally, trying to pay back taxes, over time, and learning English. If they had committed a crime, then they should be deported. But for everyone else, there must be a path to legalization. I would introduce that in the first 100 days of my presidency.

Democratic Primary Debate, University of Texas at Austin, February 21, 2008

[People are] nervous about immigration, and for the reasons that the economy isn't working for people. The average American family has lost $1,000 in income. They're looking for some explanation as to why this is happening. . . . I ask them, well, what would you do? If you want to round up and deport people, how many tens of thousands of federal law enforcement officials would that take? How much authority would they have to be given to knock on every door of every business and every home?

Democratic Primary Debate, Los Angeles, January 31, 2008

I do not think that it is appropriate to give a driver's license to someone who's here undocumented, putting them, frankly, at risk, because that is clear evidence that they are not here legally, and I believe it is a diversion from what should be the focus at creating a political coalition with the courage to stand up and change the immigration system.

Democratic Primary Debate, Los Angeles, January 31, 2008

What we have to do is bring our country together to have a comprehensive immigration reform solution. . . . If we can tighten our borders, crack down on employers who exploit workers . . . help local communities cope with the cost that they often have to contend with, if we do more to help our friends to the south create more jobs for their own people, and if we take what we know to be the realities that we confront—12 million to 14 million people here—what will we do with them? . . . For the vast majority of people who are here, we will give you a path to legalization if you meet the following conditions: Pay a fine because you entered illegally. Be willing to pay back taxes over time. Try to learn English. . . . And then you wait in line.

Democratic Primary Debate, Los Angeles, January 31, 2008

⇥ Investing in Infrastructure

We have to make investments in infrastructure. . . . This will create jobs, not only if we once again focus on our bridges, our tunnels, our ports, our airports, our mass transit—it will put millions of people to work—but it is also part of homeland security. We need to have a better infrastructure in order to protect us. And it's not only the physical infrastructure, it is the virtual infrastructure, like a national broadband system that our police and fire-fighters can actually access and use to be safe.

AFL-CIO Democratic Primary Forum, August 8, 2007

⇥ Israel

Israel is not only our ally, it is a beacon of what democracy can and should mean. . . . If the people of the Middle East are not sure what democracy means, let them look to Israel.

Speech, Yeshiva University, December 4, 2005

I love Israel and I feel so strongly about the future. . . . Israel has real problems that it has to deal with in new ways now, with all of the changes going on. I still believe it is very much in Israel's interests and Israel's security to really turn their attention to the peace process and to hammer out an agreement under appropriate safeguards for Israel's security with the Palestinian Authority.

The Atlantic, May 10, 2011

We should be looking to create an umbrella of deterrence that goes much further than just Israel. I would make it clear to the Iranians that an attack on Israel would incur massive retaliation from the United States, but I would do the same with other countries in the region.

Democratic Primary Debate, Philadelphia, April 16, 2008

⇥ Joe Biden

We've been friends for a long time and we've been on the same team. We've been on the same team in the Senate. We're on the same team now for President Obama. And no matter what I do in the future, I'd love to have Joe be on my team, because he is a great and effective person who cares deeply about our country.

CNN, May 8, 2012

⇥ John Kerry

John Kerry . . . has a very steady core. He's a man of a lot of personal strength, and he understands what it takes to lead. And because he thinks through issues and he asks questions, apparently in some quarters in American politics today, that's considered inappropriate. Whereas for me, it's very reassuring.

CBS Evening News, July 26, 2004

⊰ Keeping Her Maiden Name . . . and Changing It

It was clear that there were people who were very bothered by it. It became a kind of growing concern among his supporters, who came to see me in droves, or called me on the phone and related story after story, and said, "We really wish you would think about this." I joked one time that probably the only man in Arkansas who didn't ask me to change my name was my husband—who said, "This is your decision and you do exactly what you want." And so I did. I just decided that it was not an issue that was that big to me when it came right down to it.

Washington Post, March 10, 1992

It seemed like a sensible way of keeping my professional life separate from [Bill's] political life. I sensed that this was territory I needed to walk through pretty carefully. I did not want to be perceived as a conduit to him.

Midwest Today, June 1994

⊰ The Kind of President She'd Be

If you really look at what I've done and where I stand, I have a consistent record of standing up for people and fighting for people and getting results for people, and that's what I would do as your president.

This Week with George Stephanopoulos, May 4, 2008

When I am president, my presidency is about your future. It is about what you will have to make your lives, to make your choices however you choose, to be responsible for yourselves, those whom you love, your communities, our country and the world.

Speech, Wellesley College, November 1, 2007

⇥ Leadership

My feeling is if you're going to be a leader, you have to carefully assess where people are and where people want to go. And if that is in line with what you believe, then great; you can move in that direction and bring people along. If you've got people who are moving away from you, if you've got people who are choosing a different path, then you have to use all the tools of your suasion to try to convince them that the path that you wish to follow is also the one that is in their interest as well.

Time, October 27, 2011

You can't be a leader in the world if no one is following.

Speech, Wellesley College, November 1, 2007

⇥ Liberals

["Liberal"] is a word that originally meant that you were for freedom, for the freedom to achieve, that you were willing to stand against big power and on behalf of the individual. Unfortunately, in the last thirty, forty years, it's been turned on its head and made to seem as though it is a word that describes big government. . . . I prefer the word "progressive," which has a real American meaning, going back to the Progressive Era at the beginning of the 20th century. I consider myself a modern American progressive, someone who believes strongly in individual rights and freedoms, who believes that we are better as a society when we're working together and when we find ways to help those who may not have all the advantages in life get the tools they need to lead a more productive life for themselves and their family.

CNN/YouTube Democratic Primary Debate, July 23, 2007

⇥ Life in the White House

I don't know that anything can prepare you for ending up in the White House. It is just so many light-years apart from any other experience.

The New Yorker, October 13, 2003

If you don't stay in touch with the daily routine that most lives are made up of, it's really easy to forget what the texture of life truly is, what it's like for other people. And that's something I worry about a lot in the White House. I think it's been a great loss to our country that we have so isolated our presidents and their families.

Midwest Today, June 1994

⤙ Life's Challenges

Part of the great challenge of living is defining yourself in your moment, of seizing the opportunities that you are given, and of making the very best choices you can.

Speech, University of Texas at Austin, April 7, 1993

⤙ Lying

People can lie about you on a regular basis, and you have to take it. That's very hurtful. To see the things that are said without any refutation or correction most of the time is very painful to your friends and your family. I worry a lot about them.

Midwest Today, June 1994

I've been around long enough to know that there's often a certain level of disinformation that's going on. . . . One thing you know about me is that I have been vetted. I've been through this. I understand exactly what is coming at me, and there isn't any new information. It's just more of the same. It's been recycled over and over again. . . . My track record on being able to take on Republicans is really a proven one.

Politico, February 11, 2008

⊰⊱ Marriage

If you're married for more than ten minutes, you're going to have to forgive somebody for something.

Primetime Live, January 30, 2001

We . . . realized that a marriage between two people like us was never, ever going to be easy, if it could even happen at all.

Speech, Chautauqua Institution, June 28, 1991

I know for a long time the idea of marriage, for me, was not as clear as it certainly was for women of an earlier generation because I didn't know how it would fit in with this new personality or person that I was developing. Keeping in mind what's really important and eternal, as opposed to the mundane problems of every day that are often the things that irritate people and get them upset with each other, is really essential.

Family Circle, 1992

Talk about keeping the marriage together. . . . One of the serious issues of our marriage is that Bill Clinton does not eat chocolate.

The New York Times, December 23, 1992

In any marriage, there are issues that come up between two people that I think are their business. From my perspective, our marriage is a strong marriage. We love each other, support each other, and we have had a lot of strong and important experiences together that have meant a lot to us.

Campaign Rally, January 18, 1992

I feel very comfortable about my husband and about our marriage. We have tried to be as honest as we thought appropriate, and we have talked about who we are and where we have come from together. My view is that when you're proud of the work and effort we have put into this marriage—it is something we value very much—and it's ironic, the fact that we're married and we're willing to subject ourselves to this political process, is a subject of such concern. If Bill Clinton and I had been divorced three or four years and he were running for president, no one would ask him anything.

Newsweek, February 2, 1992

⇥ The Media

How does one keep up with the extraordinary pace of information now available? How do we make sense of that information now available? How do we make values about it even if we think we have made sense? How do we rid ourselves of the lowest common denominator that is the easiest way of conveying information?

Speech, University of Texas at Austin, April 7, 1993

⇥ The Methodist Church

I think that the Methodist Church, for a period of time, became too socially concerned, too involved in the social gospel, and did not pay enough attention to questions of personal salvation and individual faith. It is, for me, both a question of grace and of personal commitment.

Newsweek, October 30, 1994

As a Christian, part of my obligation is to take action to alleviate suffering. Explicit recognition of that in the Methodist tradition is one reason I'm comfortable in this church.

United Methodist News Service, September 16, 1992

⇥ Microcredit Programs

Microcredit is a macro idea. This is a big idea, an idea with vast potential. Whether we are talking about a rural area in South Asia or an inner-city in the U.S., microcredit is an invaluable tool in alleviating poverty. Microcredit projects can create a ripple effect—not only in lifting individuals out of poverty and moving mothers from welfare to work, but in creating jobs, promoting businesses, and building capital in depressed areas.

Speech, Microcredit Summit, February 3, 1997

⊰ The Middle East

We are always hopeful. . . . Hope springs eternal. It must, for any of us who deal with the Middle East. Otherwise, it's too depressing to contemplate.

Reuters, October 13, 2011

⊰ Midwives

That's a good idea, training midwives. Write that down. I like that. . . . I'm big on training midwives.

Reuters, October 13, 2011

⊸⊁ Military Preparedness

We can't be fighting the last war. We have to be preparing to fight the new war. We've got to be prepared to maintain the best fighting force in the world.

Speech, Veterans of Foreign Wars, August 20, 2007

⊸⊁ Modern Life

By the nature of how we spend our time today, we have walled ourselves off.... We get up in the morning and we go to work and our children don't know what our work is, because they don't see us plowing a field or making a quilt. We go off and push papers and then come home and try to explain it. Our relatives age and die often in places far away from our homes. We've compartmentalized so much of our lives that trying to find even the time to think about how all of it fits together has become harder and harder.

The New York Times Magazine, May 23, 1993

⊰∦ Her Mother

My mother, Dorothy Rodham, loved her home and her family, but she felt limited by the narrow choices of her life. It is easy to forget now, when women's choices can seem overwhelming, how few there were for my mother's generation. My mother was offended by the mistreatment of any human being, especially children. She hated self-righteousness and pretensions of moral superiority and impressed on my brothers and me that we were no better or worse than anyone else.

Living History, 2003

When I was growing up I didn't think I would run for president.... I owe the opportunity that I have here today to many people, some of whom are known to history and many who aren't. But more personally, I owe it to my mother, who never got a chance to go to college, who had a very difficult childhood, but who gave me a belief that I could do whatever I set my mind to.

Democratic Primary Debate, *This Week with George Stephanopoulos*, August 19, 2007

⊰ Her Mother-in-Law

[Bill's] mother was filled with unconditional love. You had to go so far to get her off of you. She wouldn't give up on the sorriest person you ever saw. I would sometimes have conversations with her where I would say, "Virginia, this person is"—and I would fill in the blanks. And she'd just look at me and she'd say, "Well, all I know is that he's good to his mamma," or, "He's good to his dog," or he's good to somebody. She taught me so much about love, unconditional love for people that weren't always the best that society had to offer.

Speech, National Prayer Luncheon, February 2, 1994

⊰ Motherhood

No matter how hard you try, and no matter whether you're a full-time homemaker or a full-time career woman or trying to balance both, you're going to find at times that you feel like you're not giving your child enough. That is just part of the territory of being a mother and maybe always has been.

Midwest Today, June 1994

I think that each of us does the best that we can as we learn how to be a mother, because no one is born with the instruction manual imprinted in their brain. You have to, as I told my daughter when she was a newborn baby, "I've never been a mom before and you've never been a baby before, so we just have to figure out how to do this together."

Time, May 2, 2011

Like every working mother, there's guilt involved in deciding how you're going to balance family and work. I tried to put as much time into taking care of Chelsea myself as I could. . . . I think it's a false trade-off to say quality time versus quantity—you have to have both. So if you have long work hours like I did, how do you get rid of things in your life you don't need in order to put that extra time into your children?

Marie Claire, August 24, 2007

❧ Moving to Arkansas

I had a lot of apprehension, partly because I didn't know anybody and did not know how I'd be received. . . . People were warm and welcoming to me. I felt very much at home. And it was a shock because I had never lived in the South or a small place before. It gave me a perspective on life and helped me understand what it was like for most people.

Newsweek, February 2, 1992

❧ The National Debt

We'll never accomplish what we need to do for our children if we burden them with a debt they didn't create. Franklin Roosevelt said that Americans of his generation had a rendezvous with destiny. Well, I think our generation has a rendezvous with responsibility. It's time to protect the next generation by using our budget surplus to pay down the national debt, save Social Security, modernize Medicare with a prescription drug benefit, and provide targeted tax cuts to the families who need them most.

Speech, Democratic National Convention, August 14, 2000

⤐ Needing People

There are very few people who go through life without needing anyone, without having to make any sacrifice for anyone else. In fact, it's kind of an impoverished life, if that's the attitude.

The New Yorker, October 13, 2003

⤐ New Yorkers

What it means to be a New Yorker is to be the best human being you can be, to do the best with your life you can do, to dream the biggest dreams . . . to demonstrate that we can make this wonderful patchwork quilt of a place not only work but show the rest of the world that people from different backgrounds and experiences not only can get along but build a better future.

Senate Campaign Debate, New York, October 8, 2000

New Yorkers, with their resilience, diversity and passion for the future, represent everything I treasure about America.

Living History, 2003

⇥ Nuclear Energy

I voted against Yucca Mountain in 2001. I have been consistently against Yucca Mountain. I held a hearing in the Environment Committee . . . looking at all the reasons why Yucca Mountain is not workable. The science does not support it. We do have to figure out what to do with nuclear waste. . . . I have consistently and persistently been against Yucca Mountain, and I will make sure it does not come into effect when I'm president.

Democratic Primary Debate, Las Vegas, January 15, 2008

I have a comprehensive energy plan that . . . does not rely on nuclear power. . . . I have said we should not be siting any more coal-powered plants unless they can have the most modern, clean technology. I want big demonstration projects to figure out how we would capture and sequester carbon. This is going to take a massive effort. This should be our Apollo moon shot. . . . There's work for everybody to do—the states, communities, and individuals. That's what I want to summon the country to achieve, and I think we can make it.

Democratic Primary Debate, Las Vegas, January 15, 2008

⊰⊱ Outsourcing

Outsourcing is a problem, and it's one that I've dealt with as a senator from New York. . . . We have to do several things: end the tax breaks that still exist in the tax code for outsourcing jobs, have trade agreements with enforceable labor and environmental standards, and help Americans compete.

Democratic Primary Debate, Howard University, June 28, 2007

⊰⊱ Pakistan

We have a very complex and challenging relationship with Pakistan, but we have interests that are very much in line with America's national security and Pakistani security. So we have a lot of cooperation that I think does deserve to be given some attention. We do a lot of work with the Pakistanis against terrorists. . . . But what we want to see is more cooperation from the Pakistanis themselves. . . . We don't want to open up another military conflict, and we certainly don't want to wage a war on top of the ones we are currently involved in and beginning to wrap up. . . . We get some cooperation, but not enough.

The Today Show, October 12, 2011

⊰⊱ Palestinian State

I know that it can be done. I believe that with all my heart. I feel passionately about this. This is something that is in my heart, not just in my portfolio.

The Secretary, 2013

⊰⊱ Parenting

[Parents] can resist the impulse to prove their love by showering children with things they do not need, and give them precious time and attention instead.

It Takes a Village, 1996

Let's learn from the wisdom of every mother and father all over the world who teach their daughters that there is no limit on how big she can dream and how much she can achieve. This truly is the unfinished business of the twenty-first century.

Speech, Women in the World Summit, April 5, 2013

❧ Patriotism

I am sick and tired of people who say that if you debate and you disagree with this administration, somehow you're not patriotic. We should stand up and say, "We are Americans and we have a right to debate and disagree with any administration!"

Speech, Connecticut Democratic Party Jefferson-Jackson-Bailey Day Dinner, April 28, 2003

❧ People Who Don't Vote

I'm always amazed when someone with a straight face tells me that they don't vote because they just are turned off by voting. They don't want to participate in our electoral process. And they therefore leave the entire electoral field open to people who have very different values and visions of where we are going as a country.

Speech, NAACP Annual Convention, July 11, 2000

⇥ Her Personal Philosophy

My doctrine is the Goldilocks Doctrine—not too hot, not too cold, just right.

The Atlantic, May 10, 2011

I choose my cards. I play them to the best of my ability. Move on to the next hand.

The New York Times, November 10, 2012

I always believed you could learn something from nearly everybody you meet, if you're open to it.

Hillary Rodham Clinton: A First Lady for Our Time, 1993

⊰ Her Personality

Maybe it's not as politically smart to be as direct about who you are, and what you believe in. But that's how I have always lived my life.

SFGate, February 7, 1996

⊰ Political Labels

I'm part of a growing group of people who want to get beyond those labels. They are an excuse for not thinking through problems, so that on lots of issues I'm conservative but on other issues I'm liberal. On most issues I'm somewhere in the middle trying to figure out how to get beyond all that.

Hillary Rodham Clinton: A First Lady for Our Time, 1993

I evolved my own political beliefs, which frankly, in some ways . . . weren't dogmatically Republican, dogmatically Democrat, easily defined as liberal or conservative.

Midwest Today, June 1994

⫸ Political Life

Having had political experience at this moment when politics is breaking out across the world gives me a level of empathy and understanding. I've had to talk to a lot of leaders at great length about winning and losing elections. I spent hours on the phone with [President Hamid] Karzai after his presidential election, and the fact that I could say, "Mr. President, I've won elections and I've lost elections; I do know how you feel," was an opening that most traditional diplomats just wouldn't have had the experience to be able to say.

The Economist, March 22, 2012

A political life . . . is a continuing education in human nature, including one's own.

Living History, 2003

⊰ Her Political Role

I am not a commodity. I'm a free agent. I've chosen to do what I do because I believe in it. If I didn't believe in it, I wouldn't do it.

Washington Post, March 10, 1992

My politics are a real mixture. An amalgam. And I get so amused when these people try to characterize me: "She is *this*, therefore she believes the following twenty-five things." Nobody's ever stopped to ask me or try to figure out the new sense of politics that Bill and a lot of us are trying to create. The labels are irrelevant.

Washington Post, May 6, 1993

⫸ Politics

Politics should become the art of making possible what seems impossible.

ABC News, June 8, 2003

I don't see politics as a zero-sum game where if someone's up, you're down, and vice versa. I just don't see it like that. To me, we're all part of a team.

CBS Evening News, July 26, 2004

I firmly believe that the whole purpose of politics—and it's not just elective politics on a presidential or gubernatorial level but politics with a small *p*—is how people get together, how they agree upon their goals, how they move together to realize those goals, how they make the absolutely inevitable trade-offs between deeply held beliefs that are incompatible.

Hillary Rodham Clinton: A First Lady for Our Time, 1993

At the end of the day, we have to be bigger than politics, personal politics, or partisan politics.

The Today Show, October 12, 2011

⊰╟ The Possibility of Divorce

Not only do we love each other, but we are committed to each other. That love was something so much a part of us that it was impossible to think of ending or cutting it off or moving beyond it.

Talking with David Frost, May 29, 1992

My strong feelings about divorce and its effects on children have caused me to bite my tongue more than a few times during my own marriage.

It Takes a Village, 1996

My husband and I have been husband and wife and best friends and partners for a very long time. We work together. We support each other, and I think most married couples that stay together as long as we have are in the same boat.

PBS Newshour with Jim Lehrer, May 28, 1996

⇥ Prayer

I was fortunate enough to be brought up in a home where the power of prayers was understood.

The Girls in the Van: Covering Hillary, 2001

There is just a real opportunity for people, through regular prayer and contemplation or just taking a few minutes out to think about themselves, to gain strength. And if it becomes a habit, it's always there for you. And I just hope more people, whatever their religious faith or spiritual beliefs might be, would try that. It can provide a great source of strength.

The Unique Voice of Hillary Rodham Clinton, 1997

I don't pretend to understand the wisdom and the power of God. I do believe in prayer, and I have relied on prayer consistently throughout my life. I like to say that, if I had not been a praying person before I got to the White House, after having been there for just a few days I would've become one.

Democratic Primary Debate, *This Week with George Stephanopoulos*, August 19, 2007

A very important replenisher.

Hillary: Her True Story, 1993

⊰⊱ President George W. Bush

I regret deeply that there is a Bush in the White House.

Democratic Primary Debate, Los Angeles, January 31, 2008

☙ President Obama

I think the president has done an excellent job under the most difficult circumstances. I don't think he gets the credit he deserves for making a lot of the tough decisions that he had to make that he inherited when he came into office.

The Today Show, October 12, 2011

We're both, at bottom, problem solvers and practical, realistic people. As Mario Cuomo said, "You campaign in poetry and you govern in prose."

Newsweek, April 22, 2010

☙ The Presidential Campaign

I know you think I'm nuts, but I find this exciting.

Midwest Today, June 1994

⤜ Presidential Powers

I think you have to restore the checks and balances and the separation of powers, which means reining in the presidency.

Boston Globe, October 11, 2007

⤜ Public Life

When you're in public life, you have to balance competing values.

Associated Press, March 18, 2000

The reason why we do what we do, serve in public life, is to allow for our children to reach their God-given potential.

The Secretary, 2013

⇥ Public Service

I have an old-fashioned conviction that public service is about helping people solve their problems and live their dreams. I've had every opportunity and blessing in my own life, and I want the same for all Americans. And until that day comes, you'll always find me on the front lines of democracy, fighting for the future.

Concession Speech, June 7, 2008

I don't support a draft.... We've got to look for more ways for universal national service. I've introduced legislation for a public service academy that would be patterned on great institutions like The Citadel and our military academies. Because we've got to get young people back into public service. . . . We [have] a provision in our bill . . . to have people who go into public service have their student loans deferred and even forgiven. We need to do more to support public service.

CNN/YouTube Democratic Primary Debate, July 23, 2007

⇥ Race

Race and racism are defining challenges not only in the United States but around the world. We have made progress. . . . But there is so much left to be done. And for anyone to assert that race is not a problem in America is to deny the reality in front of our very eyes. . . . We have come a long way, but, yes, we have a long way to go. The march is not finished . . . and we call on everyone to be foot soldiers in that revolution to finish the job.

Democratic Primary Debate, Howard University, June 28, 2007

We haven't always treated people in our own country fairly. We have some issues that we have to address when it comes to racial justice right now. I'm willing to work hard to be a strong advocate for civil rights and human rights here at home and around the world. I want to do everything I can to make sure that the programs and policies that have helped generations of African Americans have a better life in this country continue. I think we should be focused on the present and on the future.

We owe an apology to African Americans for hundreds of years of slavery.

New York Senate Campaign Debate, October 8, 2000

⇥ Religious Freedom

Freedom of religion does not mean, and should not mean, freedom *from* religion. And striking the appropriate balance, and being able to witness in a public role what one feels and lives through one's own spiritual journey, opens one up to misunderstanding and criticism.

Speech, National Prayer Luncheon, February 2, 1994

The search for meaning should cut across all kinds of religious and ideological boundaries. That's what we should be struggling with—not whether you have a corner on God.

Washington Post, May 6, 1993

❧ Her Religious Life

The church was a critical part of my growing up, and in preparing for this event, I almost couldn't even list all the ways it influenced me, and helped me develop as a person, not only on my own faith journey, but with a sense of obligations to others.

Speech, United Methodist Conference, April 24, 1996

One of the differences I have with some of the denominations is the idea that one's Christianity is sealed at the moment that you accept Christ as your Savior and become in whatever ways are open to you a practicing Christian. I think that is a never-ending challenge. And I believe that every day I fall short of what I should be achieving.

Newsweek, October 30, 1994

❧ Religious Responsibility

In the face of suffering, there is no doubt in my mind that
God calls us to respond.... For whatever reason it exists,
its very existence is a call to action.... The incredible
demands that God places on us ... and that Christ called
us to respond to on behalf of the poor are unavoidable.
... Maybe the Lord is just waiting for us to respond to his
call, because this despair ... is what we are expected to
be spending our time responding to, and so few of us do.
... It's a personal call; it's a family community, a religious
call, and a governmental call. And we've got to do more
to respond to that call.

Democratic Candidates Compassion Forum, Messiah College,
April 13, 2008

❧ The Religious Right

The secular press doesn't know how to talk about religion
except in stereotypes. I think they've done a great disser-
vice to many people who are in what is loosely called the

religious right. I think the people who are searching for meaning and order in their lives are naturally going to be trying to have a theology that gives them answers to difficult questions posed by modern times. I have a great deal of sympathy for that.

Newsweek, October 30, 1994

Much of the energy animating the responsible fundamentalist right has come from their sense of life getting away from us—of meaning being lost and people being turned into kind of amoral decision-makers because there weren't overriding values that they related to. And I have a lot of sympathy with that.

Washington Post, May 6, 1993

❧ Retiring as Secretary of State

I just want to sleep and exercise and travel for fun. And relax. It sounds so ordinary, but I haven't done it for twenty years. I would like to see whether I can get untired. I work out and stuff, but I don't do it enough and I don't do it hard enough because I can't expend that much energy on it.

The New York Times, November 10, 2012

⤐ Right-Wing Republicans

For fifteen years I have stood up against the right-wing machine, and I've come out stronger. So if you want a winner who knows how to take them on, I'm your girl.

AFL-CIO Democratic Primary Forum, August 8, 2007

I don't think Karl Rove's going to endorse me. That becomes more and more obvious. But I find it interesting he's so obsessed with me. And I think the reason is because we know how to win. I have been fighting against these people for longer than anybody else up here. I've taken them on and we've beaten them. . . . The idea that you're going to escape the Republican attack machine and not have high negatives by the time they're through with you, I think, is just missing what's been going on in American politics for the last twenty years.

Democratic Primary Debate, *This Week with George Stephanopoulos*, August 19, 2007

⊸❘ The Role of Government

The first priority of any government is to protect and ensure the safety of its citizens.

Speech, Yeshiva University, December 4, 2005

Competing visions of the role of government and the rights of individuals exist all along the political spectrum. Most of us hold a point of view that exists somewhere between the extremes. We may grumble about taxes, but we generally support programs like veterans' benefits, Social Security, and Medicare, along with public education, environmental protection, and some sort of social safety net for the poor. We are wary of government interference with private initiative or personal belief and the excessive influence of special interests on the political system. We respect the unique power of government to meet certain social needs and acknowledge the need to limit its powers.

It Takes a Village, 1996

I don't believe government is the source of all of our problems or the solution to them. But I do believe that when people live up to their responsibilities, we ought to live up to ours to help them build better lives. That's the basic bargain we owe one another in America today.

Campaign Announcement Speech, SUNY/Purchase, February 6, 2000

⤁ Running for President

People can overlook and ignore a whole lot of stuff that is thrown out into the atmosphere if they view it as irrelevant, tangential, or just downright stupid and nasty. If you don't have a view of the world that is bigger than yourself, if the only reason that you're doing something is to fulfill your own personal ambition, then you can't sustain a campaign against that kind of concerted attack. I think that we're ready on all those counts.

Newsweek, February 2, 1992

We come forward to the American public, and it's the most grueling political process one can imagine. We start from the same place. Nobody has an advantage, no matter who you are or where you came from. You have to raise the money. You have to make the case for yourself. I want to be judged on my own merits.

Democratic Primary Debate, Los Angeles, January 31, 2008

I was running because I thought I'd be the best president.

Concession Speech, June 7, 2008

I'm running for president to continue the work that I've done for thirty-five years. Work that is incredibly important to me that I've seen literally transform lives, from my work with the Children's Defense Fund, to fighting for change in Arkansas for better education and health care, to working in a bipartisan manner in the Senate to really solve what should be nonpartisan American problems. We have a lot of work to do. . . . I'm running for president to make it clear that we will make progress together.

Iowa Brown & Black Presidential Forum, December 1, 2007

I couldn't run as anything other than a woman. I am proud to be running as a woman. And I'm excited that I may be able, finally, to break that hardest of all glass ceilings. But, obviously, I'm not running because I'm a woman. I'm running because I think I'm the most qualified and experienced person to hit the ground running in January 2009. And I trust the American people to make a decision that is not about me or my gender . . . but about what is best for you and your family. . . . When I'm inaugurated, I think it's going to send a great message to a lot of little girls and boys around the world.

CNN/YouTube Democratic Primary Debate, July 23, 2007

⊰⊱ Russia

I don't think I can, as the president of the United States, wave my hand and tell the Russian people they should have a different government.

Boston Globe, October 11, 2007

The Russian people, like people everywhere, deserve the right to have their voices heard and their votes counted.

The New York Times Magazine, June 27, 2012

⊰⊱ Being a Senator

I just love being in the Senate. It's a wonderful experience and opportunity.

Speech, Wellesley College Reunion, June 5, 2004

I'm having the time of my life. I pinch myself every morning.

The New Yorker, October 13, 2003

The current membership of the United States Senate is not something that we can count on to protect a woman's right to choose. For women, the Senate will be our court of last resort, both because of the votes that will be taken there on issues, and because of the votes that are likely to be taken on judicial nominees. It will not be enough for any senator simply to cast the right vote and sit down.

The New York Times, January 22, 2000

This is more like a return to what I had done before those eight years [in the White House]. It has a definition; it has responsibilities. There are certain things you are expected to do. You do them to the best of your ability. So I'm very comfortable having this job.... I really have been impressed at how collegial the atmosphere is.

The New Yorker, October 13, 2003

⇥ Sitting on the Sidelines

If you do not participate, others will hijack your revolution. They will very often begin, from the first day, to undermine the hopes and aspirations that you were protesting for.

Speech, Wellesley College, June 11, 2012

⇥ Social Media

Can you imagine, in a world of Twitter, being able to sneak out of Pakistan and fly to China and do secret negotiations? It's just an entirely different 24/7 public environment that you are living in. And even if you're of a lower profile than I am, everyone around you has the technology now to report a sighting, to overhear a conversation, to snap a photo. It is an incredibly complex set of conditions that you now have to operate in at the highest levels of diplomacy anywhere.

The Economist, March 22, 2012

Given social media, given the pervasion now of commu-
nications technologies everywhere, no leader is any longer able to ignore his people.

Time, October 27, 2011

⊰⊱ Social Security

I am totally committed to making sure Social Security is
solvent. . . . You've got to begin to rein in the budget, pay
as you go, to try to replenish our Social Security Trust
Fund. And with all due respect, the last time we had a
crisis in Social Security was 1983. President Reagan and
Speaker Tip O'Neill came up with a commission. That
was the best and smartest way, because you've got to get
Republicans and Democrats together. That's what I will
do. And I will say, number one, don't cut benefits on current beneficiaries; they're already having a hard enough
time. And number two, do not impose additional tax bur-
dens on middle-class families.

Democratic Primary Debate, Philadelphia, April 16, 2008

Social Security is one of the greatest inventions in American democracy, and I will do everything possible to protect and defend it, starting with getting back to fiscal responsibility, instead of borrowing from the Social Security trust fund. We need to provide some additional opportunities for people to invest, on top of their base guarantee of Social Security, more of a chance to build their nest egg. The risky scheme to privatize would cost between $1 and $2 trillion. That would undermine the promise of Social Security.

New York Senate Primary Debate, University of Rochester, October 22, 2006

⊰⊱ Society's Promise

We need a new politics of meaning. We need a new ethos of individual responsibility and caring. We need a new definition of civil society which answers the unanswerable questions posed by both the market forces and the governmental ones, as to how we can have a society that fills us up again and makes us feel that we are part of something bigger than ourselves.

Speech, University of Texas at Austin, April 7, 1993

⊰⊱ Spreading Democracy throughout the World

I think we are always better off being on the side of democracy, but we have to keep our eyes wide open. There is no guarantee that this will be an easy road for the people themselves or, frankly, for us.

PBS Newshour with Jim Lehrer, December 14, 2011

⊰⊱ Sunday Morning News Programs

Well, I have to confess here in public. Going on the Sunday shows is not my favorite thing to do. There are other things I prefer to do on Sunday mornings. And, you know,

I haven't been on a Sunday show in way over a year. So it just isn't something I normally jump to do.

Testimony, House Foreign Affairs Committee, January 23, 2013

⊰≫ Taking Action

I can't stand whining. I can't stand the kind of paralysis that some people fall into because they're not happy with the choices they've made. You live in a time when there are endless choices. . . . Money certainly helps, and having that kind of financial privilege goes a long way, but you don't even have to have money for it. But you have to work on yourself. . . . Do something!

Marie Claire, October 18, 2012

⊰ Taking Naps

Sleep has taken a back seat. I told Bill we have a budget deficit, an investment deficit, and a sleep deficit. I believe with Churchill that naps are a restorative.

The New York Times, February 2, 1993

⊰ Tax Reform

I am absolutely committed to not raising a single tax on middle class Americans, people making less than $250,000 a year.

Democratic Primary Debate, Philadelphia, April 16, 2008

I don't want to raise taxes on anybody.

Democratic Primary Debate, Philadelphia, April 16, 2008

ᐅᗁ The Tea Party

To address the issues that are paramount today, [we need] effectively functioning governments. There are those who insist on assaulting government, who claim that if we would only abolish or severely weaken it that everyone's freedom and prosperity would blossom. That is, I believe, a very mistaken notion. We need strong and efficient governments—not oppressive or weak ones—that are able to empower citizens to help them take responsibility for their families and communities.

Speech, The Sorbonne, Paris, June 17, 1999

ᐅᗁ Technology

Technology, from satellite television to cell phones, from Twitter to Tumblr, is helping bring abuses out of the shadows and into the center of global consciousness. Think of that woman in a blue bra beaten in Tahrir Square, think about that six-year-old girl in Afghanistan about to be sold into marriage to settle a family debt. Just as importantly, technological changes are helping inspire, organize, and empower grassroots action. I have seen this and that is where progress is coming from and that's where our support is needed. We have a tremendous stake in the outcome of these metrics.

Speech, Women in the World Summit, April 5, 2013

⫸ Terrorism

The stateless terrorists will operate from somewhere. Part of our message has to be there is no safe haven. If we can demonstrate that the people responsible for planning the nuclear attack on our country may not themselves be in a government or associated with a state, but have a haven within one, then every state in the world must know we will retaliate against those states. . . . We have to make it clear to those states that would give safe haven to stateless terrorists that would launch a nuclear attack against America that they would also face a very heavy retaliation.

Democratic Primary Debate, January 5, 2008

The war on terrorism is a long-term challenge, and
. . . it will be important to understand what our military response will be and to satisfy myself we're as well
defended as we need to be.

The New Yorker, October 13, 2003

⊹ Toxic Substances

We don't do anywhere near enough to try to prevent
dangerous materials and products from coming into our
country. We don't even do enough of it within our own
country. We have totally turned our back on the information that is available to try to better track the impact
on children and others of these kinds of exposures to
toxic materials. So, number one, we need tougher standards across the board, something I've been advocating
for years. Number two, it should be especially applied to
any kind of imports, and that requires going and making
sure that we have inspectors on the ground and we have
tough standards and we exercise recalls.

Democratic Candidates' Debate, National Public Radio,
December 4, 2007

⇥ Travel

You would think in the twenty-first century where we have instantaneous communication, where I can have a videoconference halfway around the world, that you wouldn't be expected to travel as much. But in fact, I think people want you to show up even more. America has to show up, and I very proudly represent our country when I show up. So being on that airplane, making those visits, having those negotiations and discussions is a very demanding part of the job, but necessary.

The Today Show, October 12, 2011

⇥ The Value of Art

I believe strongly that art should be accessible to everyone, because it has the power to evoke in each of us a deeper understanding of our lives and of the world around us.

Speech, The Sculpture Garden Reception at the White House, January 5, 1996

It is particularly ironic that those who bemoan the loss of civility and character and the loss of values in America are the first to recommend obliterating the federal agencies, in many ways cutting back on state and local support, responsible for promoting our cultural traditions.

Speech, Metropolitan Museum of Art, June 6, 1995

⚛ Her Values

I've gone from a Barry Goldwater Republican to a New Democrat, but I think my underlying values have remained pretty constant: individual responsibility and community—I don't see those as mutually inconsistent.

New York Magazine, April 3, 2000

⚛ Voting

I have a new theory: I think if you don't vote, you should lose the right to complain. I'm going to start telling people, "If you didn't want to vote, I don't want to hear about the pothole, I don't want to hear the problem with some other program."

The New York Times, November 6, 2000

We heard firsthand from people in Cleveland who had been disenfranchised, all the people who waited for ten or twelve hours because the precincts they were in only had two voting machines, whereas down the road, in a more affluent and whiter precinct, people could vote in a couple of minutes. We need to end the disparities in resources. We need to have same-day voter registration and earlier absentee voting. We need to make it clear that we'd like to try a holiday or a weekend for voting because more people will be able to get off work and actually do it. And we need to end the oppressive ID requirements that are turning people away from the polls and restore the voting rights of ex-felons.

Democratic Primary Forum, NAACP, July 12, 2007

✺ Wal-Mart

It's a mixed blessing. . . . When Wal-Mart started, it brought goods into rural areas, like rural Arkansas where I was happy to live for eighteen years, and gave people a chance to stretch their dollar further. As they grew much bigger, though, they have raised serious questions about the responsibility of corporations and how they need to be a leader when it comes to providing health care and having safe working conditions and not discriminating on the basis of sex or race.

Democratic Primary Debate, South Carolina, April 26, 2007

✺ Watching HGTV's *Love It or List It*

I find it very calming.

The New York Times, November 10, 2012

❧ The Welfare of Women

If women are healthy and educated, their families will flourish. If women are free from violence, their families will flourish. If women have a chance to work and earn as full and equal partners in society, their families will flourish. And when families flourish, communities and nations will flourish.

Speech, United Nations Fourth World Conference on Women, September 5, 1995

❧ What She'd Like to Do as President

I have a million ideas. The country can't afford them all.

Boston Globe, October 11, 2007

⧈ Why Richard Nixon Attacked Her in the 1992 Campaign

[Nixon] was launching a preemptive attack to try and in some way to denigrate my husband because he's unafraid of smart and intelligent women and really believes that women ought to have opportunities to serve.

Hillary Rodham Clinton: A First Lady for Our Time, 1993

⧈ WikiLeaks

Let's be clear. This disclosure is not just an attack on America—it's an attack on the international community. There is nothing laudable about endangering innocent people, and there is nothing brave about sabotaging the peaceful relations between nations.

National Public Radio, November 29, 2010

➤ Women and Washington

American women don't need lectures from Washington about values. We don't need to hear about an idealized world that was never as righteous or carefree as some would like to think.

Commencement Speech, Wellesley College, May 29, 1992

➤ Women in Politics

There's such a dearth of women leaders in the vast majority of countries, including our own, that there isn't any doubt that empowering women in poor countries—[and] in undemocratic countries—would make a significant difference in increasing the stability of those societies. We need to recognize that, and encourage more women to run at all levels for elective office, and to be in positions to take appointed office such as secretary of state and federal judges. We need to do more to create the pipeline for women from both the public and private sector to be able to have a greater increase to get a critical mass, beyond the 14 percent to 20 percent that we seem to be stuck at.

Speech, Wellesley College, June 5, 2004

⊰ Women Who Play Dumb

When I got into high school, I saw a lot of my friends who had been really lively and smart and doing well in school beginning to worry that boys would think they were too smart, or beginning to cut back on how well they did or the courses they took, because that's not where their boyfriends were. And I can recall thinking, "Gosh—why are they doing that?" It didn't make sense to me.

Washington Post, March 10, 1992

There's that kind of double bind that women find themselves in. On the one hand, yes, be smart, stand up for yourself. On the other hand, don't offend anybody, don't step on toes, or you'll become somebody that nobody likes because you're too assertive.

Midwest Today, June 1994

⇥ Women's Diversity

We need to understand there is no formula for how women should lead their lives. That is why we must respect the choices that each woman makes for herself and her family. Every woman deserves the chance to realize her own God-given potential.

Speech, United Nations Fourth World Conference on Women, September 5, 1995

⇥ Women's Insecurities

The only thing that is holding women back from realizing their full potential is their own insecurity about the choices they make in their own lives and their unwillingness to listen to the silent voice inside themselves which tells them what is the right decision for them.

Speech, Scripps College, April 26, 1994

⚘ Women's Rights

The world is changing beneath our feet and it is past time to embrace a twenty-first-century approach to advancing the rights and opportunities of women and girls at home and across the globe.

Speech, Women in the World Summit, April 5, 2013

⚘ Women's Roles

I have always believed that women are not victims, we are agents of change, we are drivers of progress, we are makers of peace—all we need is a fighting chance.

Speech, Women in the World Summit, April 5, 2013

There is no doubt in my mind that without the involvement of women in the economy, in politics, in peacemaking, in every aspect of society, you can't realize [a country's] full potential.

Marie Claire, October 18, 2012

⊰ Her Work Style

[I] just keep at it, take it piece by piece, seize the ground you can, hang on to it, and then move forward a little bit more.

Newsweek, March 6, 2011

You get up every day and you get out there and you make your case, and you reach as many people as possible.

This Week with George Stephanopoulos, December 30, 2007

I'm one of these very focused people when it comes to day-to-day work, and I'm trying not to think about what comes next so that I can stay very focused on what I'm doing now.

The Economist, March 22, 2012

I think I'm very hardheaded. I've never understood the division between so-called realists and so-called idealists. I don't know how you get up in the world every day, doing what I do, if you don't have some sense of idealism, because you have to believe that as hard as it is, you're going to prevent the dictator from oppressing his people, you're going to help to stop the war, you're going to figure out a way to get clean water to thirsty people and cure kids of disease. And at the same time, I don't know how you go through the day and expect to be successful without being very hardheaded and realistic. So for me, it's not an either/or.

The Atlantic, May 10, 2011

⊰ Working with President Obama

It is such a key relationship that you really have to invest time and effort in it. . . . But at the end of the day, it's that sort of funnel; the tough decisions end up in the Oval Office. And you can't just walk in and say to the president, "Here's what I think you should do." It takes a lot of thought and effort. I meet with the president one-on-one once a week. I'm in other meetings with him with the national-security team. It's a constant conversation.

Newsweek, December 20, 2009

Sources

ABORTION

"I am and always . . .": Adam Nagourney, "Hillary Clinton Vows to Fight to Preserve Abortion Rights," *The New York Times*, January 22, 2000, http://www.nytimes.com/2000/01/22/nyregion/hillary-clinton-vows-to -fight-to-preserve-abortion-rights.html.

"I've been saying . . .": Joanna Coles, "Hillary Clinton Unplugged," *Marie Claire*, August 24, 2007, http://www.marieclaire.com/world-reports /news/hillary-clinton-interview.

"Forces are aligned . . .": Speech, NARAL, January 22, 2004.

"I think abortion should . . .": Democratic Candidates Compassion Forum, Messiah College, April 13, 2008, http://transcripts.cnn.com /TRANSCRIPTS/0804/13/se.01.html.

"I have met thousands . . .": Speech, NARAL, January 22, 1999.

AGE

"I feel so relieved . . .": *Political Ticker* (blog), CNN, May 8, 2012, http://politi
calticker.blogs.cnn.com/2012/05/08/clinton-addresses-au-naturale
-moment/.

AGRICULTURAL POLICY

"We have to have . . .": Democratic Primary Debate, *This Week with George
Stephanopoulos*, ABC, August 19, 2007, http://a.abcnews.com/Politics
/Decision2008/story?id=3498294&page=17.

AMERICA

"I believe our values . . .": Interview with Savannah Guthrie, *The Today
Show*, NBC, October 12, 2011, http://www.state.gov/secretary/rm/2011/10
/175861.htm.

"We always led . . .": Richard Stengel, "Q&A: Hillary Clinton on Libya,
China, the Middle East and Barack Obama," *Time*, October 27, 2011,
http://swampland.time.com/2011/10/27/qa-hillary-clinton-on-libya
-china-the-middle-east-and-barack-obama/.

"We have a system . . .": Donnie Radcliffe, *Hillary Rodham Clinton: A First
Lady for Our Time* (New York: Grand Central Publishing, 1999), 109.

AMERICAN LEADERSHIP

"We do have to keep innovating . . .": Speech, Joint Civilian Service Award
Presentation, February 14, 2013, http://hillaryclintonoffice.com/.

"I think when you inherit . . .": Michael Hirsh, "Obama's Bad Cop,"
Newsweek, April 22, 2010, http://www.thedailybeast.com/newsweek/2010
/04/22/obama-s-bad-cop.html.

The American Political System

"What's great about our . . .": Democratic Primary Debate, Los Angeles, January 31, 2008, http://www.nytimes.com/2008/01/31/us/politics/31text -debate.html.

America's Greatest Threat

"The greatest threat . . .": Richard Stengel, "Q&A: Hillary Clinton on Libya, China, the Middle East and Barack Obama," *Time*, October 27, 2011, http://swampland.time.com/2011/10/27/qa-hillary-clinton-on-libya -china-the-middle-east-and-barack-obama/.

America's Role in the World

"Our country is not only . . .": Interview with Savannah Guthrie, *The Today Show*, NBC, October 12, 2011, http://www.state.gov/secretary/rm/2011/10 /175861.htm.

"I cannot tell you . . .": Interview with Reuters, October 13, 2011, http:// www.state.gov/secretary/rm/2011/10/175374.htm.

"We can't just walk out . . .": Michael Hirsh, "Obama's Bad Cop," *Newsweek*, April 22, 2010, http://www.thedailybeast.com/newsweek/2010/04/22/ obama-s-bad-cop.html.

"The United States can't solve . . .": Steven Lee Myers, "Hillary Clinton's Last Tour as a Rock-Star Diplomat," *The New York Times Magazine*, June 27, 2012, http://www.nytimes.com/2012/07/01/magazine/hillary-clintons -last-tour-as-a-rock-star-diplomat.html.

"The United States bears . . .": Kim Ghattas, *The Secretary: A Journey with Hillary Clinton from Beirut to the Heart of American Power* (New York: Times Books, 2013), 227.

Her Appearance

"If I want to knock . . .": Bob Cohn and Bill Turque, "Hillary Shores Up a Shaky Base for '96," *Newsweek*, June 4, 1995, http://www.thedailybeast .com/newsweek/1995/06/04/hillary-shores-up-a-shaky-base-for-96.html.

"Everything I said or did . . .": Hillary Clinton, *Living History* (New York: Simon & Schuster, 2003), 111.

Asia

"We do see Asia . . .": Kim Ghattas, *The Secretary: A Journey with Hillary Clinton from Beirut to the Heart of American Power* (New York: Times Books, 2013), 31.

Balancing Your Life

"Most of us will . . .": Joanna Coles, "Hillary Clinton Unplugged," *Marie Claire*, August 24, 2007, http://www.marieclaire.com/world-reports /news/hillary-clinton-interview.

"The first lesson I've learned . . .": Ibid.

Becoming a Grandmother

"Let me just say . . .": Interview with George Stephanopoulos, *Good Morning America*, January 18, 2011, http://www.state.gov/secretary /rm/2011/01/154920.htm.

Being Secretary of State

"The work that I tried . . .": "An Interview with Hillary Clinton," *Lexington's Notebook* (blog), *The Economist*, March 22, 2012, http://www.economist .com/blogs/lexington/2012/03/foreign-policy.

"It's never the same...": Interview with Savannah Guthrie, *The Today Show*, NBC, October 12, 2011, http://www.state.gov/secretary/rm/2011 /10/175861.htm.

"What I have found...": Jon Meacham, "Meeting of the Diplomats," *Newsweek*, December 20, 2009, http://www.thedailybeast.com/newsweek /2009/12/20/meeting-of-the-diplomats.html.

"One of my goals...": Richard Stengel, "Q&A: Hillary Clinton on Libya, China, the Middle East and Barack Obama," *Time*, October 27, 2011, http://swampland.time.com/2011/10/27/qa-hillary-clinton-on-libya -china-the-middle-east-and-barack-obama/.

"Part of my mission...": Ibid.

"There might be times...": *PBS Newshour with Jim Lehrer*, PBS, December 14, 2011, http://www.pbs.org/newshour/rundown/2011/12/clinton -interview.html.

"It's an impossible job...": Interview with Savannah Guthrie, *The Today Show*, NBC, October 12, 2011, http://www.state.gov/secretary/rm/2011 /10/175861.htm.

BEING TRUE TO HERSELF

"You have to be...": Ayelet Waldman, "Is This Really Goodbye?" *Marie Claire*, October 18, 2012, http://www.marieclaire.com/world-reports /inspirational-women/hillary-clinton-farewell.

THE BIBLE

"If I quote...": Kenneth L. Woodward, "Soulful Matters," *Newsweek*, October 30, 1994, http://www.thedailybeast.com/newsweek/1994/10/30 /soulful-matters.html.

"Ever since I was . . .": Democratic Compassion Forum, Messiah College, April 13, 2008, http://transcripts.cnn.com/TRANSCRIPTS/0804/13/se.01 .html.

"Matthew 5, 6 and 7 . . .": Kenneth L. Woodward, "Soulful Matters," *Newsweek*, October 30, 1994, http://www.thedailybeast.com/newsweek /1994/10/30/soulful-matters.html.

BILL CLINTON AS A FATHER

"[Bill] was amazed by . . .": Eleanor Clift, "I Think We're Ready," *Newsweek*, February 2, 1992, http://www.thedailybeast.com/newsweek/1992/02/02 /i-think-we-re-ready.html.

BILL CLINTON AS FIRST HUSBAND

"He will not have . . .": Interview with George Stephanopoulos, *This Week with George Stephanopoulos*, ABC, December 30, 2007, http://abcnews.go .com/blogs/politics/2007/12/bill-clinton-ba/.

BIPARTISANSHIP IN WASHINGTON

"Too often in Washington . . .": Haley Daniels, "Hillary Clinton in AJU Lecture Says Reaching Across the Aisle Like Negotiating with Terrorists," *Huffington Post*, June 26, 2013, http://www.huffingtonpost.com/2013/06/26 /hillary-clinton-aju-lecture_n_3499404.html.

"Whether you're on . . .": Interview with Savannah Guthrie, *The Today Show*, NBC, October 12, 2011, http://www.state.gov/secretary/rm/2011/10 /175861.htm.

"You've got to get . . .": Democratic Primary Debate, Philadelphia, April 16, 2008, http://www.nytimes.com/2008/04/16/us/politics/16text-debate .html.

BUILDING RELATIONSHIPS WITH OTHER COUNTRIES

"I think it's important . . .": Interview with Savannah Guthrie, *The Today Show*, NBC, October 12, 2011, http://www.state.gov/secretary/rm/2011/10 /175861.htm.

CAMPAIGN FINANCE REFORM

"We need public financing . . .": George Stephanopoulos, *This Week with George Stephanopoulos*, ABC, December 30, 2007, http://abcnews.go.com /blogs/politics/2007/12/bill-clinton-ba/.

"I'm very much in favor . . .": *Meet the Press*, NBC, September 23, 2007, http://www.issues2000.org/Archive/2008_Meet_the_Press_Government _Reform.htm.

"There is this artificial distinction . . .": Democratic Primary Debate, *This Week with George Stephanopoulos*, ABC, August 19, 2007, http://a.abcnews .com/Politics/Decision2008/story?id=3498294&page=17.

HER CHANCES TO WIN THE PRESIDENCY

"I believe that both . . .": Marcella Bombardieri, "Clinton Vows to Check Executive Power," *Boston Globe*, October 11, 2007, http://www.boston.com /news/nation/articles/2007/10/11/clinton_vows_to_check_executive _power/.

CHEF ALICE WATERS

"I think she's been . . .": Marian Burros, "Hillary Clinton's New Home: Broccoli's In, Smoking's Out," *The New York Times*, February 2, 1993, http:// www.nytimes.com/1993/02/02/us/hillary-clinton-s-new-home-broccoli -s-in-smoking-s-out.html.

Her Childhood

"When I was a little younger . . .": Interview with Barbara Walters, ABC News, June 8, 2003, http://votesmart.org/public-statement/9701/# .Uhex9mRgZIg.

"I never felt anything . . .": Donnie Radcliffe, *Hillary Rodham Clinton: A First Lady for Our Time* (New York: Grand Central Publishing, 1993), 35.

Children

"We cannot permit . . .": Speech, United Methodist General Conference, April 24, 1996, http://gbgm-umc.org/umw/bible/hilltext.stm.

China

"We will continue . . .": Interview with Hu Shuli and Huang Shan of Caixin Media Company, May 11, 2011, http://www.state.gov/secretary /rm/2011/05/163022.htm.

"We don't walk away . . .": Jeffrey Goldberg, "Hillary Clinton: Chinese System Is Doomed, Leaders on a 'Fool's Errand,'" *The Atlantic*, May 10, 2011, http://www.theatlantic.com/international/archive/2011/05/hillary -clinton-chinese-system-is-doomed-leaders-on-a-fools-errand/238591/.

"China . . . [is] still by any standard . . .": Interview with Reuters, October 11, 2011, http://www.state.gov/secretary/rm/2011/10/175374.htm.

"We are two different . . .": Interview with Hu Shuli and Huang Shan of Caixin Media Company, May 11, 2011, http://www.state.gov/secretary /rm/2011/05/163022.htm.

HER COMMUNICATION STYLE

"With every tough message . . .": Michael Hirsh, "Obama's Bad Cop." *Newsweek*, April 22, 2010, http://www.thedailybeast.com/newsweek/2010/04/22/obama-s-bad-cop.html.

COMMUNISM

"We would always be engaged . . .": Donnie Radcliffe, *Hillary Rodham Clinton: A First Lady for Our Time* (New York: Grand Central Publishing, 1993), 25.

COMMUNITY

"Why is it in a country . . .": Speech, Liz Carpenter Lecture Series, University of Texas at Austin, April 7, 1993, http://clinton3.nara.gov/WH/EOP/First_Lady/html/generalspeeches/1993/19930407.html.

CORPORATE AMERICA

"Corporate America today . . .": Democratic Primary Debate, South Carolina, April 26, 2007, http://www.wistv.com/Global/story.asp?s=6434957.

CRIME

"We have to do . . .": Democratic Primary Debate, Howard University, June 28, 2007, http://www.nytimes.com/2007/06/28/us/politics/29transcript.html.

"We will never build . . .": *SFGate*, February 7, 1996, http://www.sfgate.com/news/article/HILLARY-CLINTON-IN-HER-OWN-WORDS-3151660.php.

Her Critics

"If I worried . . .": Larry Jordan, "The Real Hillary Clinton," *Midwest Today*, June 1994, http://www.midtod.com/highlights/hillary.phtml.

"Why would they spend . . .": Donnie Radcliffe, *Hillary Rodham Clinton: A First Lady for Our Time* (New York: Grand Central Publishing, 1993), 7.

"I was amused . . .": Speech, National Prayer Luncheon, February 2, 1994, http://clinton4.nara.gov/media/text/1994-02-02-first-lady-remarks-to -the-national-prayer-luncheon.text.

"It would be hard . . .": George Stephanopoulos, *This Week with George Stephanopoulos*, ABC, December 29, 2007, http://abcnews.go.com/blogs /politics/2007/12/bill-clinton-ba/.

"You always get angry . . .": Donnie Radcliffe, *Hillary Rodham Clinton: A First Lady for Our Time* (New York: Grand Central Publishing, 1993), 237–38.

"I learned a long time ago . . .": Larry Jordan, "The Real Hillary Clinton," *Midwest Today*, June 1994, http://www.midtod.com/highlights/hillary .phtml.

Daily Life

"From my perspective . . .": George Stephanopoulos, *This Week with George Stephanopoulos*, ABC, December 29, 2007, http://abcnews.go.com/blogs /politics/2007/12/bill-clinton-ba/.

"I just take it . . .": Gail Sheehy, "Hillaryland at War," *Vanity Fair*, August 2008, http://www.vanityfair.com/politics/features/2008/08/clinton 200808.

Her Daughter

"I am just bursting . . .": Official Swearing-In Ceremony as Secretary of State, February 2, 2009, http://www.state.gov/secretary/rm/2009a /02/115841.htm.

"I think she does have . . .": Interview with Savannah Guthrie, *The Today Show*, NBC, October 12, 2011, http://www.state.gov/secretary/rm/2011/10 /175861.htm.

"I have tried very hard . . .": Eleanor Clift, "I Think We're Ready," *Newsweek*, February 2, 1992, http://www.thedailybeast.com/newsweek/1992/02/02/ i-think-we-re-ready.html.

The Democratic Party

"The Democratic Party is . . .": Concession Speech, June 7, 2008, http:// www.nytimes.com/2008/06/07/us/politics/07text-clinton.html.

"Time and time again . . .": Interview with Leon Harris, *Politico*, February 11, 2008, http://www.politico.com/news/stories/0208/8459.html.

The District of Columbia

"I want to get . . .": Interview with Leon Harris, *Politico*, February 11, 2008, http://www.politico.com/news/stories/0208/8459.html.

The Economy

"Some think that the market . . .": Speech, The Sorbonne, Paris, June 17, 1999.

"I believe that the foundation . . .": Take Back America Conference, June 20, 2007, http://www.dailykos.com/story/2007/09/03/380128/-Hillary-rsquo -s-Statement-On-Labor-Day.

"I will turn this economy . . .": Democratic Primary Debate, Philadelphia, April 16, 2008, http://www.nytimes.com/2008/04/16/us/politics/16text-debate.html.

EDUCATION

"I'm a strong supporter . . .": Democratic Primary Debate, Philadelphia, April 16, 2008, http://www.nytimes.com/2008/04/16/us/politics/16text-debate.html.

"We also know that . . .": Student Commencement Speech, Wellesley College, May 31, 1969, http://www.cbsnews.com/2100-250_162-3448588.html.

"I support school-based merit pay . . .": Democratic Primary Debate, Las Vegas, November 15, 2007, http://transcripts.cnn.com/TRANSCRIPTS/0711/15/se.02.html.

"I know there are some . . .": Speech, National Education Association, Orlando, July 5, 1999, http://clinton2.nara.gov/WH/EOP/First_Lady/html/generalspeeches/1999/19990705.html.

"I think teachers are . . .": New York Senate Debate, October 28, 2000.

"What we're trying to do . . .": Democratic Primary Debate, *This Week with George Stephanopoulos*, ABC, August 19, 2007, http://a.abcnews.com/Politics/Decision2008/story?id=3498294&page=17.

"I don't think merit pay . . .": Adam Nagourney, "School Cuts Are an 'Admission of Failure,' Mrs. Clinton Says, *The New York Times*, April 6, 2000, http://www.nytimes.com/2000/04/06/nyregion/school-cuts-are-an-admission-of-failure-mrs-clinton-says.html.

The Education of Women

"Educating young women...": Kim Ghattas, *The Secretary: A Journey with Hillary Clinton from Beirut to the Heart of American Power* (New York: Times Books, 2013), 135.

Empowerment

"I've spent a lifetime...": Democratic Primary Debate, Philadelphia, April 16, 2008, http://www.nytimes.com/2008/04/16/us/politics/16text -debate.html.

Energy Policy

"If we have $4 gas...": Democratic Primary Debate, Philadelphia, April 16, 2008, http://www.nytimes.com/2008/04/16/us/politics/16text -debate.html.

English as the "Official" Language

"It is important that...": Democratic Primary Debate, University of Texas at Austin, February 21, 2008, http://www.ontheissues.org/Archive/Archive _TX_Immigration.htm.

Equal Pay

"Equal pay is not...": Democratic Primary Debate, Congressional Black Caucus Institute, January 21, 2008, http://www.cnn.com/2008/POLITICS /01/21/debate.transcript/.

Evil

"There are evil people...": Michael Kelly, "Saint Hillary," *The New York Times Magazine*, May 23, 1993, http://www.nytimes.com/1993/05/23 /magazine/saint-hillary.html.

FACING CHALLENGES

"You know, in life . . .": Gail Sheehy, "Hillaryland at War," *Vanity Fair*, August 2008, http://www.vanityfair.com/politics/features/2008/08/clinton200808.

"The most difficult decisions . . .": Hillary Clinton, *Living History* (New York: Simon & Schuster, 2003), 506.

FAITH

"I am an old-fashioned . . .": Kenneth L. Woodward, "Soulful Matters," *Newsweek*, October 30, 1994, http://www.thedailybeast.com/newsweek/1994/10/30/soulful-matters.html.

"I was raised with faith . . .": Interview with Barbara Walters, ABC News, June 8, 2003, http://votesmart.org/public-statement/9701/#.Uhex9mRgZIg.

"You have to fight . . .": *Live with Regis and Kathie Lee*, June 10, 1996.

"We know that acting . . .": Speech, United Methodist General Conference, April 24, 1996, http://gbgm-umc.org/umw/bible/hilltext.stm.

"Faith is something . . .": Speech, National Prayer Luncheon, February 2, 1994, http://clinton4.nara.gov/media/text/1994-02-02-first-lady-remarks-to-the-national-prayer-luncheon.text.

"In the world . . .": Donnie Radcliffe, *Hillary Rodham Clinton: A First Lady for Our Time* (New York: Grand Central Publishing, 1993), 262.

HER FATHER

"My dad, Hugh Rodham . . .": Hillary Clinton, *Living History* (New York: Simon & Schuster, 2003), 11.

FEMINISM

"I am a woman . . .": Concession Speech, June 7, 2008, http://
www.nytimes.com/2008/06/07/us/politics/07text-clinton.html.

FIGHTING

"You show people . . .": Cabinet and Staff Retreat at Camp David, January
1993, http://www.usnews.com/news/articles/2007/01/30/10-things-you
-didnt-know-about-hillary-clinton.

"The harder they hit . . .": Hillary Clinton, *The Unique Voice of Hillary
Rodham Clinton*, ed. Claire G. Osborne (New York: Avon, 1996), 74.

BEING FIRST LADY

"There's nothing comparable . . .": Elizabeth Kolbert, "The Student," *The
New Yorker*, October 13, 2003, http://www.newyorker.com/archive/2003/10
/13/031013fa_fact_kolbert.

"I know that no matter . . .": Michael Kelly, "Saint Hillary," *The New York
Times Magazine*, May 23, 1993, http://www.nytimes.com/1993/05/23
/magazine/saint-hillary.html.

FOREIGN AID

"In Congress, there are some . . .": Interview with Reuters, October 13, 2011,
http://www.state.gov/secretary/rm/2011/10/175374.htm.

FOREIGN POLICY

"There will be times . . .": Kim Ghattas, *The Secretary: A Journey with Hillary
Clinton from Beirut to the Heart of American Power* (New York: Times
Books, 2013), 324.

"We now understand . . .": Ibid., 336.

"What was possible for . . .": Richard Stengel, "Q&A: Hillary Clinton on Libya, China, the Middle East and Barack Obama," *Time*, October 27, 2011, http://swampland.time.com/2011/10/27/qa-hillary-clinton-on-libya-china -the-middle-east-and-barack-obama/.

FORGIVENESS

"[The gift of forgiveness] . . .": Speech, National Prayer Luncheon, February 2, 1994, http://clinton4.nara.gov/media/text/1994-02-02-first -lady-remarks-to-the-national-prayer-luncheon.text.

FREE TRADE

"We've got to have . . .": AFL-CIO Democratic Primary Forum, August 8, 2007, http://www.nytimes.com/2007/08/08/us/politics/07demsforum .html.

"Trade needs to become . . .": Democratic Primary Debate, *This Week with George Stephanopoulos*, ABC, August 19, 2007, http://a.abcnews.com /Politics/Decision2008/story?id=3498294&page=17.

FREEDOM

"Americans believe that . . .": Kim Ghattas, *The Secretary: A Journey with Hillary Clinton from Beirut to the Heart of American Power* (New York: Times Books, 2013), 324.

THE FUTURE

"The kind of help . . .": Kim Ghattas, *The Secretary: A Journey with Hillary Clinton from Beirut to the Heart of American Power* (New York: Times Books, 2013), 336.

GAY RIGHTS AND MARRIAGE

"Being gay is not...": Speech, International Human Rights Day, Geneva, Switzerland, December 6, 2011, http://www.state.gov/secretary/rm/2011/12/178368.htm.

"Gay rights are human rights...": Ibid.

"I support it personally...": Speech, Human Rights Campaign Video, March 18, 2013, http://www.washingtonpost.com/blogs/post-partisan/wp/2013/03/18/hillary-clinton-officially-says-yes-to-gay-marriage/.

GOD

"I think God...": Kenneth L. Woodward, "Soulful Matters," *Newsweek*, October 30, 1994, http://www.thedailybeast.com/newsweek/1994/10/30/soulful-matters.html.

"I have, ever since...": Democratic Candidates Compassion Forum, Messiah College, April 13, 2008, http://transcripts.cnn.com/TRANSCRIPTS/0804/13/se.01.html.

GOVERNMENT CRONYISM

"Let's start by cleaning...": Take Back America Conference, June 20, 2007, http://www.dailykos.com/story/2007/09/03/380128/-Hillary-rsquo-s-Statement-On-Labor-Day.

"How about the radical idea...": Ibid.

GOVERNMENT SURVEILLANCE VERSUS THE RIGHT TO PRIVACY

"Unchecked mass surveillance...": Associated Press, June 16, 2006, http://www.democraticunderground.com/discuss/duboard.php?az=view_all&address=102x2341856.

GOVERNMENT TRANSPARENCY

"I want to have . . .": *Meet the Press*, NBC, January 13, 2008, http://
www.issues2000.org/Archive/2008_Meet_the_Press_Government
_Reform.htm.

THE GOVERNMENT'S ROLE IN FAMILY

"No government can love . . .": Speech, Child Welfare League, March 1, 1995.

HER GUILTY PLEASURE

"When I get tired . . .": Speech, Conference on "Power: Women as Drivers
of Growth and Social Inclusion," Lima, Peru, October 16, 2012, http://
www.state.gov/secretary/rm/2012/10/199209.htm.

GUN CONTROL

"I respect the Second Amendment . . .": Democratic Primary Debate,
Philadelphia, April 16, 2008, http://www.nytimes.com/2008/04/16/us
/politics/16text-debate.html.

"If you own a gun . . .": *Good Morning America*, June 4, 1999.

"We have to do everything . . .": Speech, National Education Association,
Orlando, July 5, 1999, http://clinton2.nara.gov/WH/EOP/First_Lady/html
/generalspeeches/1999/19990705.html.

"I am against illegal guns . . .": Democratic Primary Debate, Las Vegas,
January 15, 2008, http://www.lasvegassun.com/news/2008/jan/15
/debate-transcript/.

Her Health

"I am, thankfully . . .": "Barbara Walters Presents: The 10 Most Fascinating People of 2012," ABC News, December 12, 2012, http://abcnews.go.com/Politics/hillary-clinton-reveals-thoughts-secretary-state-2016-hair/story?id=17943370.

How People Perceive Her

"Sometimes it is hard . . .": Talking It Over, Creators Syndicate, August 1, 2001, http://www.creators.com/opinion/hillary-clinton/talking-it-over-1995-07-23.html.

"I'm a Rorschach test . . .": Walter Shapiro, "Whose Hillary Is She Anyway?" *Esquire*, August 1993.

"It seemed that people . . .": Hillary Clinton, *Living History* (New York: Simon & Schuster, 2003), 140–41.

How She Does Her Job

"I would not be . . .": Kim Ghattas, *The Secretary: A Journey with Hillary Clinton from Beirut to the Heart of American Power* (New York: Times Books, 2013), 313.

"At the end of the day . . .": Michael Hirsh, "Obama's Bad Cop," *Newsweek*, April 22, 2010, http://www.thedailybeast.com/newsweek/2010/04/22/obama-s-bad-cop.html.

"I think I understand . . .": Interview with Savannah Guthrie, *The Today Show*, NBC, October 12, 2011, http://www.state.gov/secretary/rm/2011/10/175861.htm.

How She Views America

"I would ask that . . .": Kim Ghattas, *The Secretary: A Journey with Hillary Clinton from Beirut to the Heart of American Power* (New York: Times Books, 2013) 330.

"I see America as . . .": Ibid., 329.

How She Views Herself

"I'm smart . . .": Donnie Radcliffe, *Hillary Rodham Clinton: A First Lady for Our Time* (New York: Grand Central Publishing, 1993), 52.

Her Husband

"I am so grateful . . .": Official Swearing-In Ceremony as Secretary of State, February 2, 2009, http://www.state.gov/secretary/rm/2009a/02 /115841.htm.

"What he's really done . . .": Larry Jordan, "The Real Hillary Clinton," *Midwest Today*, June 1994, http://www.midtod.com/highlights/hillary .phtml.

"To this day . . .": Hillary Clinton, *Living History* (New York: Simon & Schuster, 2003), 53–54.

"He's also genuinely optimistic . . .": Larry Jordan, "The Real Hillary Clinton," *Midwest Today*, June 1994, http://www.midtod.com/highlights /hillary.phtml.

"No one understands me . . .": Hillary Clinton, *Living History* (New York: Simon & Schuster, 2003), 75.

"I'm very lucky . . .": Kim Ghattas, *The Secretary: A Journey with Hillary Clinton from Beirut to the Heart of American Power* (New York: Times Books, 2013), 40.

Her Husband's Political Accomplishments

"I'm very proud . . .": Democratic Primary Debate, Los Angeles, January 31, 2008, http://www.nytimes.com/2008/01/31/us/politics/31text-debate .html.

Her Husband's Role in Her Presidency

"There are two roles . . .": Interview with Leon Harris, *Politico*, February 11, 2008, http://www.politico.com/news/stories/0208/8459.html.

"He'll play a very important . . .": *Fox News Sunday with Chris Wallace*, February 3, 2008, http://www.foxnews.com/story/2008/02/03/transcript -hillary-clinton-on-fox-news-sunday/.

Immigration Policy

"As president, I would work . . .": Democratic Primary Debate, University of Texas at Austin, February 21, 2008, http://www.ontheissues.org/Archive /Archive_TX_Immigration.htm.

"[People are] nervous about . . .": Democratic Primary Debate, Los Angeles, January 31, 2008, http://www.nytimes.com/2008/01/31/us/politics/31text -debate.html.

"I do not think that . . .": Ibid.

"We have to bring our country . . .": Ibid.

Investing in Infrastructure

"We have to make . . .": AFL-CIO Democratic Primary Forum, August 8, 2007, http://www.nytimes.com/2007/08/08/us/politics/07demsforum .html.

ISRAEL

"Israel is not only . . .": Speech, Yeshiva University, December 4, 2005, http://www.villagevoice.com/2005-12-06/news/hillary-calls-israel-a -beacon-of-democracy/full/.

"I love Israel . . .": Jeffrey Goldberg, "Hillary Clinton: Chinese System Is Doomed, Leaders on a 'Fool's Errand,'" *The Atlantic*, May 10, 2011, http:// www.theatlantic.com/international/archive/2011/05/hillary-clinton -chinese-system-is-doomed-leaders-on-a-fools-errand/238591/.

"We should be looking . . .": Democratic Primary Debate, Philadelphia, April 16, 2008, http://www.nytimes.com/2008/04/16/us/politics/16text -debate.html.

JOE BIDEN

"We've been friends . . .": Interview with Jill Dougherty, CNN, Delhi, May 8, 2012, http://www.state.gov/secretary/rm/2012/05/189459.htm.

JOHN KERRY

"John Kerry . . . has a very . . .": Interview with Dan Rather, *CBS Evening News*, July 26, 2004, http://www.cbsnews.com/8301-18563_162-631937.html.

KEEPING HER MAIDEN NAME . . . AND CHANGING IT

"It was clear . . .": Lloyd Grove, "Hillary Clinton, Trying to Have It All," *Washington Post*, March 10, 1992.

"It seemed like a sensible way . . .": Larry Jordan, "The Real Hillary Clinton," *Midwest Today*, June 1994, http://www.midtod.com/highlights/hillary .phtml.

The Kind of President She'd Be

"If you really look . . .": *This Week with George Stephanopoulos*, ABC, May 4, 2008, http://abcnews.go.com/ThisWeek/story?id=4783456.

"When I am president . . .": Speech, Wellesley College, November 1, 2007, http://www.presidency.ucsb.edu/ws/index.php?pid=77072.

Leadership

"My feeling is . . .": Richard Stengel, "Q&A: Hillary Clinton on Libya, China, the Middle East and Barack Obama," *Time*, October 27, 2011, http://swamp land.time.com/2011/10/27/qa-hillary-clinton-on-libya-china-the-middle -east-and-barack-obama/.

"You can't be . . .": Speech, Wellesley College, November 1, 2007, http://www.presidency.ucsb.edu/ws/index.php?pid=77072.

Liberals

"['Liberal'] is a word . . .": CNN/YouTube Democratic Primary Debate, Charleston, South Carolina, July 23, 2007, http://www.cnn.com/2007 /POLITICS/07/23/debate.transcript/.

Life in the White House

"I don't know that . . .": Elizabeth Kolbert, "The Student," *The New Yorker*, October 13, 2003, http://www.newyorker.com/archive/2003/10/13/031013 fa_fact_kolbert.

"If you don't stay . . .": Larry Jordan, "The Real Hillary Clinton," *Midwest Today*, June 1994, http://www.midtod.com/highlights/hillary.phtml.

Life's Challenges

"Part of the great challenge . . .": Speech, Liz Carpenter Lecture Series, University of Texas at Austin, April 7, 1993, http://clinton3.nara.gov/WH /EOP/First_Lady/html/generalspeeches/1993/19930407.html.

Lying

"People can lie . . .": Larry Jordan, "The Real Hillary Clinton," *Midwest Today*, June 1994, http://www.midtod.com/highlights/hillary.phtml.

"I've been around . . .": Interview with Leon Harris, *Politico*, February 11, 2008, http://www.politico.com/news/stories/0208/8459.html.

Marriage

"If you're married . . .": *Primetime Live*, ABC, January 30, 2001.

"We . . . realized that . . .": Speech, Chautauqua Institution, June 28, 1991.

"I know for a long . . .": Marian Burros, *Family Circle*, 1992.

"Talk about keeping . . .": Marian Burros, "Bill Clinton and Food: Jack Sprat He's Not," *The New York Times*, December 23, 1992.

"In any marriage . . .": Campaign rally, January 18, 1992, http://articles .chicagotribune.com/1992-01-26/news/9201080326_1_hillary-clinton -bill-clinton-gennifer-flowers.

"I feel very comfortable . . .": Eleanor Clift, "I Think We're Ready," *Newsweek*, February 2, 1992, http://www.thedailybeast.com/newsweek/1992/02/02 /i-think-we-re-ready.html.

The Media

"How does one . . .": Speech, Liz Carpenter Lecture Series, University of Texas at Austin, April 7, 1993, http://clinton3.nara.gov/WH/EOP/First _Lady/html/generalspeeches/1993/19930407.html.

The Methodist Church

"I think that . . .": Kenneth L. Woodward, "Soulful Matters," *Newsweek*, October 30, 1994, http://www.thedailybeast.com/newsweek/1994/10/30 /soulful-matters.html.

"As a Christian . . .": Jean Caffey Lyles, "Hillary Clinton: Wesley's Theology Fits Her Life," United Methodist News Service, September 16, 1992.

Microcredit Programs

"Microcredit is a macro idea . . .": Speech, Microcredit Summit, Washington, DC, February 3, 1997.

The Middle East

"We are always hopeful . . .": Interview with Reuters, October 13, 2011, http://www.state.gov/secretary/rm/2011/10/175374.htm.

Midwives

"That's a good idea . . .": Interview with Reuters, October 13, 2011, http:// www.state.gov/secretary/rm/2011/10/175374.htm.

Military Preparedness

"We can't be fighting . . .": Speech, Veterans of Foreign Wars, Kansas City, Missouri, August 20, 2007.

MODERN LIFE

"By the nature . . .": Michael Kelly, "Saint Hillary," *The New York Times Magazine*, May 23, 1993, http://www.nytimes.com/1993/05/23/magazine /saint-hillary.html.

HER MOTHER

"My mother, Dorothy Rodham . . .": Hillary Clinton, *Living History* (New York: Simon & Schuster, 2003), 10–11.

"When I was growing up . . .": Democratic Primary Debate, *This Week with George Stephanopoulos*, ABC, August 19, 2007, http://a.abcnews.com /Politics/Decision2008/story?id=3498294&page=17.

HER MOTHER-IN-LAW

"[Bill's] mother was filled . . .": Speech, National Prayer Luncheon, February 2, 1994, http://clinton4.nara.gov/media/text/1994-02-02-first -lady-remarks-to-the-national-prayer-luncheon.text.

MOTHERHOOD

"No matter how hard . . .": Larry Jordan, "The Real Hillary Clinton," *Midwest Today*, June 1994, http://www.midtod.com/highlights/hillary.phtml.

"I think that each . . .": Interview with Belinda Luscombe, *Time*, May 2, 2011, http://www.state.gov/secretary/rm/2011/04/162340.htm.

"Like every working mother . . .": Joanna Coles, "Hillary Clinton Unplugged," *Marie Claire*, August 24, 2007, http://www.marieclaire.com /world-reports/news/hillary-clinton-interview.

MOVING TO ARKANSAS

"I had a lot of apprehension . . .": Eleanor Clift, "I Think We're Ready," *Newsweek*, February 2, 1992, http://www.thedailybeast.com/newsweek /1992/02/02/i-think-we-re-ready.html.

THE NATIONAL DEBT

"We'll never accomplish . . .": Speech, Democratic National Convention, August 14, 2000, http://www.pbs.org/newshour/election2000/demcon vention/hillary_8-14.htm.

NEEDING PEOPLE

"There are very few . . .": Elizabeth Kolbert, "The Student," *The New Yorker*, October 13, 2003, http://www.newyorker.com/archive/2003/10/13/031013 fa_fact_kolbert.

NEW YORKERS

"What it means . . .": Senate Campaign Debate, New York, October 8, 2000, http://www.nytimes.com/2000/10/09/nyregion/campaign-2000-new -york-senate-debate-excerpts-second-debate-between-mrs-clinton.html.

"New Yorkers, with their . . .": Hillary Clinton, *Living History* (New York: Simon & Schuster, 2003), 508.

NUCLEAR ENERGY

"I voted against Yucca Mountain . . .": Democratic Primary Debate, Las Vegas, January 15, 2008, http://www.lasvegassun.com/news/2008/jan/15 /debate-transcript/.

"I have a comprehensive energy plan . . .": Ibid.

Outsourcing

"Outsourcing is a problem . . .": Democratic Primary Debate, Howard University, June 28, 2007, http://www.nytimes.com/2007/06/28/us/politics/29transcript.html.

Pakistan

"We have a very complex . . .": Interview with Savannah Guthrie, *The Today Show*, NBC, October 12, 2011, http://www.state.gov/secretary/rm/2011/10/175861.htm.

Palestinian State

"I know that it can . . .": Kim Ghattas, *The Secretary: A Journey with Hillary Clinton from Beirut to the Heart of American Power* (New York: Times Books, 2013), 71.

Parenting

"[Parents] can resist the impulse . . .": Hillary Clinton, *It Takes a Village* (New York: Simon & Schuster, 1996), 292.

"Let's learn from the wisdom . . .": Speech, Women in the World Summit, April 5, 2013, http://hillaryclintonoffice.com/.

Patriotism

"I am sick and tired . . .": Speech, Connecticut Democratic Party Jefferson-Jackson-Bailey Day Dinner, April 28, 2003.

People Who Don't Vote

"I'm always amazed . . .": Speech, NAACP Annual Convention, July 11, 2000, http://abcnews.go.com/Politics/story?id=123402.

Her Personal Philosophy

"My doctrine . . .": Jeffrey Goldberg, "Hillary Clinton: Chinese System Is Doomed, Leaders on a 'Fool's Errand,'" *The Atlantic*, May 10, 2011, http://www.theatlantic.com/international/archive/2011/05/hillary-clinton-chinese-system-is-doomed-leaders-on-a-fools-errand/238591/.

"I choose my cards . . .": Gail Collins, "Hillary's Next Move," *The New York Times*, November 10, 2012, http://www.nytimes.com/2012/11/11/opinion/sunday/collins-hillarys-next-move.html.

"I always believed . . .": Donnie Radcliffe, *Hillary Rodham Clinton: A First Lady for Our Time* (New York: Grand Central Publishing, 1993), 259.

Her Personality

"Maybe it's not as politically . . .": *SFGate*, February 7, 1996, http://www.sfgate.com/news/article/HILLARY-CLINTON-IN-HER-OWN-WORDS-3151660.php.

Political Labels

"I'm part of a . . .": Donnie Radcliffe, *Hillary Rodham Clinton: A First Lady for Our Time* (New York: Grand Central Publishing, 1993), 254–55.

"I evolved my own . . .": Larry Jordan, "The Real Hillary Clinton," *Midwest Today*, June 1994, http://www.midtod.com/highlights/hillary.phtml.

Political Life

"Having had political experience . . .": "An Interview with Hillary Clinton," *Lexington's Notebook* (blog), *The Economist*, March 22, 2012, http://www.economist.com/blogs/lexington/2012/03/foreign-policy.

"A political life . . ." Hillary Clinton, *Living History* (New York: Simon & Schuster, 2003), x.

Her Political Role

"I am not a commodity . . .": Lloyd Grove, "Hillary Clinton, Trying to Have It All," *Washington Post*, March 10, 1992.

"My politics are a real mixture . . .": Martha Sherrill, "Hillary Clinton's Inner Politics," *Washington Post*, May 6, 1993.

Politics

"Politics should become . . .": Interview with Barbara Walters, ABC News, June 8, 2003, http://votesmart.org/public-statement/9701/# .Uhex9mRgZIg.

"I don't see politics . . .": Interview with Dan Rather, *CBS Evening News*, July 26, 2004, http://www.cbsnews.com/8301-18563_162-631937.html.

"I firmly believe . . .": Donnie Radcliffe, *Hillary Rodham Clinton: A First Lady for Our Time* (New York: Grand Central Publishing, 1993), 24.

"At the end of the day . . .": Interview with Savannah Guthrie, *The Today Show*, NBC, October 12, 2011, http://www.state.gov/secretary/rm/2011 /10/175861.htm.

The Possibility of Divorce

"Not only do we . . .": *Talking with David Frost*, May 29, 1992.

"My strong feelings . . .": Hillary Clinton, *It Takes a Village* (New York: Simon & Schuster, 1996), 43.

"My husband and I . . .": *PBS Newshour with Jim Lehrer*, PBS, May 28, 1996, http://www.pbs.org/newshour/bb/white_house/jan-june96/hillary clinton_05-28.html.

PRAYER

"I was fortunate enough . . .": Beth Harpaz, *The Girls in the Van: Covering Hillary* (New York: St. Martin's Press, 2001), 195.

"There is just . . .": Hillary Clinton, *The Unique Voice of Hillary Rodham Clinton*, ed. Claire G. Osborne (New York: Avon Books, 1997), 88–90.

"I don't pretend to understand . . .": Democratic Primary Debate, *This Week with George Stephanopoulos*," ABC, August 19, 2007, http://a.abcnews.com /Politics/Decision2008/story?id=3498294&page=17.

"A very important replenisher . . .": Norman King, *Hillary: Her True Story* (New York: Birch Lane Press, 1993), 8.

PRESIDENT GEORGE W. BUSH

"I regret deeply . . .": Democratic Primary Debate, Los Angeles, January 31, 2008, http://www.nytimes.com/2008/01/31/us/politics/31text-debate .html.

PRESIDENT OBAMA

"I think the president . . .": Interview with Savannah Guthrie, *The Today Show*, NBC, October 12, 2011, http://www.state.gov/secretary/rm/2011 /10/175861.htm.

"We're both, at bottom . . .": Michael Hirsh, "Obama's Bad Cop," *Newsweek*, April 22, 2010, http://www.thedailybeast.com/newsweek/2010/04/22 /obama-s-bad-cop.html.

THE PRESIDENTIAL CAMPAIGN

"I know you think . . .": Larry Jordan, "The Real Hillary Clinton," *Midwest Today*, June 1994, http://www.midtod.com/highlights/hillary.phtml.

PRESIDENTIAL POWERS

"I think you have . . .": Marcella Bombardieri, "Clinton Vows to Check Executive Power," *Boston Globe*, October 11, 2007, http://www.boston.com/news/nation/articles/2007/10/11/clinton_vows_to_check_executive_power/.

PUBLIC LIFE

"When you're in public life . . .": Beth Harpaz, "Hillary Clinton Booed at Parade," Associated Press, March 18, 2000.

"The reason why we do . . .": Kim Ghattas, *The Secretary: A Journey with Hillary Clinton from Beirut to the Heart of American Power* (New York: Times Books, 2013), 91.

PUBLIC SERVICE

"I have an old-fashioned . . .": Concession speech, June 7, 2008, http://www.nytimes.com/2008/06/07/us/politics/07text-clinton.html.

"I don't support a draft . . .": CNN/YouTube Democratic Primary Debate, Charleston, South Carolina, July 23, 2007, http://www.cnn.com/2007/POLITICS/07/23/debate.transcript/.

RACE

"Race and racism . . .": Democratic Primary Debate, Howard University, June 28, 2007, http://www.nytimes.com/2007/06/28/us/politics/29transcript.html.

"We haven't always treated . . .": New York Senate Campaign Debate, October 8, 2000, http://vote-ny.org/politicianissue.aspx?state=ny&id=nyclintonhillaryrodham&issue=busminorities.

Religious Freedom

"Freedom of religion . . .": Speech, National Prayer Luncheon, February 2, 1994, http://clinton4.nara.gov/media/text/1994-02-02-first-lady-remarks -to-the-national-prayer-luncheon.text.

"The search for meaning . . .": Martha Sherrill, "Hillary Clinton's Inner Politics," *Washington Post*, May 6, 1993.

Her Religious Life

"The church was a critical part . . .": Speech, United Methodist Conference, April 24, 1996, http://gbgm-umc.org/umw/bible/hilltext.stm.

"One of the differences . . .": Kenneth L. Woodward, "Soulful Matters," *Newsweek*, October 30, 1994, http://www.thedailybeast.com/ newsweek/1994/10/30/soulful-matters.html.

Religious Responsibility

"In the face of suffering . . .": Democratic Candidates Compassion Forum, Messiah College, April 13, 2008, http://transcripts.cnn.com/TRANSCRIPTS /0804/13/se.01.html.

The Religious Right

"The secular press . . .": Kenneth L. Woodward, "Soulful Matters," *Newsweek*, October 30, 1994, http://www.thedailybeast.com/newsweek /1994/10/30/soulful-matters.html.

"Much of the energy animating . . .": Martha Sherrill, "Hillary Clinton's Inner Politics," *Washington Post*, May 6, 1993.

Retiring as Secretary of State

"I just want to sleep . . .": Gail Collins, "Hillary's Next Move," *The New York Times*, November 10, 2012, http://www.nytimes.com/2012/11/11/opinion/sunday/collins-hillarys-next-move.html.

Right-Wing Republicans

"For fifteen years . . .": AFL-CIO Democratic Primary Forum, August 8, 2007, http://www.nytimes.com/2007/08/08/us/politics/07demsforum.html.

"I don't think Karl Rove's . . .": Democratic Primary Debate, *This Week with George Stephanopoulos*, ABC, August 19, 2007, http://a.abcnews.com/Politics/Decision2008/story?id=3498294&page=17.

The Role of Government

"The first priority . . .": Speech, Yeshiva University, December 4, 2005, http://www.villagevoice.com/2005-12-06/news/hillary-calls-israel-a-beacon-of-democracy/full/.

"Competing visions of the role . . .": Hillary Clinton, *It Takes a Village* (New York: Simon & Schuster, 1996), 286.

"I don't believe government . . .": Campaign Announcement Speech, SUNY/Purchase, February 6, 2000.

Running for President

"People can overlook . . .": Eleanor Clift, "I Think We're Ready," *Newsweek*, February 2, 1992, http://www.thedailybeast.com/newsweek/1992/02/02/i-think-we-re-ready.html.

"We come forward...": Democratic Primary Debate, Los Angeles, January 31, 2008, http://www.nytimes.com/2008/01/31/us/politics /31text-debate.html.

"I was running because...": Concession Speech, June 7, 2008, http:// www.nytimes.com/2008/06/07/us/politics/07text-clinton.html.

"I'm running for president...": Iowa Brown & Black Presidential Forum, December 1, 2007, http://www.bbpresforum.org/transcript.html.

"I couldn't run as anything...": CNN/YouTube Democratic Primary Debate, Charleston, South Carolina, July 23, 2007, http://www.cnn.com /2007/POLITICS/07/23/debate.transcript/.

Russia

"I don't think I can...": Marcella Bombardieri, "Clinton Vows to Check Executive Power," *Boston Globe*, October 11, 2007, http://www.boston .com/news/nation/articles/2007/10/11/clinton_vows_to_check _executive_power/

"The Russian people...": Steven Lee Myers, "Hillary Clinton's Last Tour as a Rock-Star Diplomat," *The New York Times Magazine*, June 27, 2012, http://www.nytimes.com/2012/07/01/magazine/hillary-clintons-last -tour-as-a-rock-star-diplomat.html.

Being a Senator

"I just love...": Speech, Wellesley College Reunion, June 5, 2004.

"I'm having the time...": Elizabeth Kolbert, "The Student," *The New Yorker*, October 13, 2003, http://www.newyorker.com/archive/2003/10/13/0310 13fa_fact_kolbert.

"The current membership...": Adam Nagourney, "Hillary Clinton Vows to Fight to Preserve Abortion Rights," *The New York Times*, January 22, 2000,

http://www.nytimes.com/2000/01/22/nyregion/hillary-clinton-vows-to
-fight-to-preserve-abortion-rights.html.

"This is more . . .": Elizabeth Kolbert, "The Student," *The New Yorker*,
October 13, 2003, http://www.newyorker.com/archive/2003/10/13
/031013fa_fact_kolbert.

SITTING ON THE SIDELINES

"If you do not participate . . .": Speech, Wellesley College, June 11, 2012,
http://www.boston.com/yourtown/news/wellesley/2012/06/secretary
_of_state_hillary_cli.html.

SOCIAL MEDIA

"Can you imagine . . .": "An Interview with Hillary Clinton," *Lexington's
Notebook* (blog), *The Economist*, March 22, 2012, http://www.economist
.com/blogs/lexington/2012/03/foreign-policy.

"Given social media . . .": Richard Stengel, "Q&A: Hillary Clinton on Libya,
China, the Middle East and Barack Obama," *Time*, October 27, 2011,
http://swampland.time.com/2011/10/27/qa-hillary-clinton-on-libya-china
-the-middle-east-and-barack-obama/.

SOCIAL SECURITY

"I am totally committed . . .": Democratic Primary Debate, Philadelphia,
April 16, 2008, http://www.nytimes.com/2008/04/16/us/politics/16text
-debate.html.

"Social Security is one . . .": New York Senate Primary Debate, University of
Rochester, October 22, 2006.

Society's Promise

"We need a new politics . . .": Speech, Liz Carpenter Lecture Series, University of Texas at Austin, April 7, 1993, http://clinton3.nara.gov/WH /EOP/First_Lady/html/generalspeeches/1993/19930407.html.

Spreading Democracy throughout the World

"I think we are always . . .": *PBS Newshour with Jim Lehrer*, PBS, December 14, 2011, http://www.pbs.org/newshour/rundown/2011/12/clinton -interview.html.

Sunday Morning News Programs

"Well, I have to confess . . .": Testimony, House Foreign Affairs Committee, January 23, 2013, http://www.politico.com/blogs/media/2013/01/clinton -sunday-shows-not-my-favorite-thing-to-do-155046.html.

Taking Action

"I can't stand whining . . .": Ayelet Waldman, "Is This Really Goodbye?" *Marie Claire*, October 18, 2012, http://www.marieclaire.com/world-reports /inspirational-women/hillary-clinton-farewell.

Taking Naps

"Sleep has taken . . .": Marian Burros, "Hillary Clinton's New Home: Broccoli's In, Smoking's Out," *The New York Times*, February 2, 1993, http://www.nytimes.com/1993/02/02/us/hillary-clinton-s-new-home -broccoli-s-in-smoking-s-out.html.

TAX REFORM

"I am absolutely committed . . .": Democratic Primary Debate, Philadelphia, April 16, 2008, http://www.nytimes.com/2008/04/16/us /politics/16text-debate.html.

"I don't want to . . .": Ibid.

THE TEA PARTY

"To address the issues . . .": Speech, The Sorbonne, Paris, June 17, 1999.

TECHNOLOGY

"Technology, from satellite television . . .": Speech, Women in the World Summit, April 5, 2013, http://hillaryclintonoffice.com/.

TERRORISM

"The stateless terrorists . . .": Democratic Primary Debate, WMUR-NH, January 5, 2008, http://www.nytimes.com/2008/01/05/us/politics /05text-ddebate.html.

"The war on terrorism . . .": Elizabeth Kolbert, "The Student," *The New Yorker*, October 13, 2003, http://www.newyorker.com/archive/2003/10/13 /031013fa_fact_kolbert.

TOXIC SUBSTANCES

"We don't do anywhere . . .": Democratic Candidates' Debate, National Public Radio, December 4, 2007, http://www.npr.org/templates/story /story.php?storyId=16898435.

Travel

"You would think . . .": Interview with Savannah Guthrie, *The Today Show*, NBC, October 12, 2011, http://www.state.gov/secretary/rm/2011/10/175861.htm.

The Value of Art

"I believe strongly . . .": Speech, The Sculpture Garden Reception at the White House, January 5, 1996.

"It is particularly ironic . . .": Speech, Metropolitan Museum of Art, June 6, 1995.

Her Values

"I've gone from . . .": Michael Tomasky and Mary Ellen Mark, "Hillary's Turn," *New York Magazine*, April 3, 2000, http://www.maryellenmark.com/text/magazines/new_york_magazine/906C-000-004.html.

Voting

"I have a new theory . . .": Adam Nagourney, "Entering Last Act, Senate Rivals Stick to the Script," *The New York Times*, November 6, 2000, http://www.nytimes.com/2000/11/06/nyregion/entering-last-act-senate-rivals-stick-script-mrs-clinton-preaches-party-faithful.html.

"We heard firsthand . . .": Democratic Primary Forum, NAACP, July 12, 2007.

Wal-Mart

"It's a mixed blessing . . .": Democratic Primary Debate, South Carolina, April 26, 2007, http://www.wistv.com/Global/story.asp?s=6434957.

Watching HGTV's *Love It or List It*

"I find it . . .": Gail Collins, "Hillary's Next Move," *The New York Times*, November 10, 2012, http://www.nytimes.com/2012/11/11/opinion/sunday /collins-hillarys-next-move.html.

The Welfare of Women

"If women are healthy . . .": Speech, United Nations Fourth World Conference on Women, September 5, 1995, http://clinton4.nara.gov/WH /EOP/First_Lady/html/9-5-95.html.

What She'd Like to Do as President

"I have a million ideas . . .": Marcella Bombardieri, "Clinton Vows to Check Executive Power," *Boston Globe*, October 11, 2007, http://www.boston .com/news/nation/articles/2007/10/11/clinton_vows_to_check _executive_power/.

Why Richard Nixon Attacked Her in the 1992 Campaign

"[Nixon] was launching . . .": Donnie Radcliffe, *Hillary Rodham Clinton: A First Lady for Our Time* (New York: Grand Central Publishing, 1993), 9.

WikiLeaks

"Let's be clear . . .": Scott Neuman, "Clinton: WikiLeaks 'Tear at Fabric' of Government," National Public Radio, November 29, 2010, http://www.npr .org/2010/11/29/131668950/white-house-aims-to-limit-wikileaks-damage.

Women and Washington

"American women don't need . . .": Commencement Speech, Wellesley College, May 29, 1992, http://www.apnewsarchive.com/1992/

Hillary-Clinton-Decries-Lectures-From-Washington-To-Women/id-b56
460e1511b47834a3bb070adcf68dd.

Women in Politics

"There's such a dearth . . .": Speech, Wellesley College, June 5, 2004.

Women Who Play Dumb

"When I got into high school . . .": Lloyd Grove, "Hillary Clinton, Trying to
Have It All," *Washington Post*, March 10, 1992.

"There's that kind of . . .": Larry Jordan, "The Real Hillary Clinton," *Midwest
Today*, June 1994, http://www.midtod.com/highlights/hillary.phtml.

Women's Diversity

"We need to understand . . .": Speech, United Nations Fourth World
Conference on Women, September 5, 1995, http://clinton4.nara.gov/WH
/EOP/First_Lady/html/9-5-95.html.

Women's Insecurities

"The only thing . . .": Speech, Scripps College, April 26, 1994, http://clinton4
.nara.gov/media/text/1994-04-26-first-lady-keynote-address-at-scripps
-college.text.

Women's Rights

"The world is changing . . .": Speech, Women in the World Summit, April 5,
2013, http://hillaryclintonoffice.com/.

WOMEN'S ROLES

"I have always believed . . .": Speech, Women in the World Summit, April 5, 2013, http://hillaryclintonoffice.com/.

"There is no doubt . . .": Ayelet Waldman, "Is This Really Goodbye?" *Marie Claire*, October 18, 2012, http://www.marieclaire.com/world-reports /inspirational-women/hillary-clinton-farewell.

HER WORK STYLE

"[I] just keep at it . . .": Gayle Tzemach Lemmon, "The Hillary Doctrine," *Newsweek*, March 6, 2011, http://www.thedailybeast.com/newsweek/2011 /03/06/the-hillary-doctrine.html.

"You get up every day . . .": *This Week with George Stephanopoulos*, ABC, December 29, 2007, http://abcnews.go.com/blogs/politics/2007/12/bill -clinton-ba/.

"I'm one of these . . .": "An Interview with Hillary Clinton," *Lexington's Notebook* (blog), *The Economist*, March 22, 2012, http://www.economist .com/blogs/lexington/2012/03/foreign-policy.

"I think I'm very hardheaded . . .": Jeffrey Goldberg, "Hillary Clinton: Chinese System Is Doomed, Leaders on a 'Fool's Errand,'" *The Atlantic*, May 10, 2011, http://www.theatlantic.com/international/archive/2011 /05/hillary-clinton-chinese-system-is-doomed-leaders-on-a-fools-errand /238591/.

WORKING WITH PRESIDENT OBAMA

"It is such a key relationship . . .": Jon Meacham, "Meeting of the Diplomats," *Newsweek*, December 20, 2009, http://www.thedailybeast .com/newsweek/2009/12/20/meeting-of-the-diplomats.html.

Selected Titles from Seal Press

What Will It Take to Make a Woman President?: Conversations about Women, Leadership, and Power, by Marianne Schnall. $16.00, 978-1-58005-496-6. This timely discussion features interviews with more than twenty leading politicians, writers, artists, and activists about why America has not yet elected a female president.

Full Frontal Feminism: A Young Woman's Guide to Why Feminism Matters, by Jessica Valenti. $15.95, 978-1-58005-201-6. A sassy and in-your-face look at contemporary feminism for women of all ages.

No Excuses: 9 Ways Women Can Change How We Think about Power, by Gloria Feldt. $18.00, 978-1-58005-388-4. From the boardroom to the bedroom, public office to personal relationships, feminist icon Gloria Feldt offers women the tools they need to walk through the doors of opportunity and achieve parity with men.

Intimate Politics: How I Grew Up Red, Fought for Free Speech, and Became a Feminist Rebel, by Bettina F. Aptheker. $16.95, 978-1-58005-160-6. A courageous and uncompromising account of one woman's personal and political transformation, and a fascinating portrayal of a key chapter in our nation's history.

Get Opinionated: A Progressive's Guide to Finding Your Voice (and Taking A Little Action), by Amanda Marcotte. $15.95, 978-1-58005-302-0. Hilarious, bold, and very opinionated, this book helps young women get a handle on the issues they care about—and provides suggestions for the small steps they can take towards change.

Find Seal Press Online
www.SealPress.com
www.Facebook.com/SealPress
Twitter: @SealPress